The
Man Who...

The Man Who...

The Story of the 1932 Democratic National Convention

by Richard Oulahan

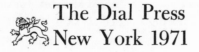 The Dial Press
New York 1971

Library of Congress Catalog Card Number: 78-131186
Printed in the United States of America
Book design by Stuart Rosenberg
First printing, 1971

TO ANNE

And to Carroll, Dick, Molly, Dennis,
Tony, Pepe, Anne, and the others

ACKNOWLEDGMENTS

The author is grateful to James A. Farley, Arthur Krock, David Lawrence, and George Allen, all participants in or observers of the 1932 Democratic Convention, for generous and valuable help in furnishing information for this book.

Since most of the material for the book was gleaned from histories, memoirs, unpublished papers, and published periodicals, indebtedness is acknowledged to librarians and staff assistants at the New York Public Library and its Periodicals Branch; the Bridgeport Library, Bridgeport, Connecticut; the Pequot Library, Southport, Connecticut; the Westport Library, Westport, Connecticut; the Wilton Library, Wilton, Connecticut; the Library of Congress, Washington, D. C.; the Benjamin Franklin Library, Casa Americana, Madrid; and especially the Franklin D. Roosevelt Library, Hyde Park, New York, and its librarian, Elizabeth B. Drewry.

Louise Samuels, Lea Guyer, Carroll Sweet, the author's daughter, and the late Eleanor Darnton, all contributed useful research or suggestions. Special thanks are due to A. L. Hart, Jr., the publisher, who conceived the idea for this volume, and Phyllis Jackson, for her encouragement and help in steering the book to publication. Finally, the author owes a particular debt to his wife, Anne Regan Oulahan, for helping in the research, critiquing the manuscript, correcting the spelling, and for patiently spending so much of her time over the past two years in the distant days of 1932.

CONTENTS

Chapter 1   A Time of Violence and Despair   1

Chapter 2   The Republican Decade   8

Chapter 3   The *Presidenciables*   14

Chapter 4   Blueprint for a Campaign   25

Chapter 5   First Blood: The Primaries   39

Chapter 6   The Republican Convention   57

Chapter 7   The Eve of Battle   66

Chapter 8   "We Have Roosevelt Licked Now"   71

Chapter 9   The Debacle of the Two-Thirds Rule   80

Chapter 10   The Struggle Over the Permanent Chairmanship   87

Chapter 11   Prohibition and the Platform   92

Chapter 12   Deadlock   104

Chapter 13   The Switch that Made History   114

Chapter 14   "A New Deal for the American People"   131

Afterword   139

Bibliography   141

Index   143

CHAPTER 1

A TIME
OF VIOLENCE
AND DESPAIR

On a pleasant May morning in 1932, a mad Russian fatally shot the President of France as he signed autographs at a Paris book fair. A few weeks later, young soldiers and sailors, the henchmen of Japan's militant warlords, invaded the home of the premier of Japan and assassinated him in his own living room for the crime of being a peaceable man. In South America, Bolivia and Paraguay were locked in a bloody war for possession of Gran Chaco, a tract of worthless jungle. And in Moscow, the young wife of the dictator, Josef Stalin, died of a bullet wound, by her own hand, or those of her husband's hired assassins.

It was a time of violence and hatred, unrest and despair. The thunderheads of imminent revolution and chaos raced across a dozen nations, from Spain to Siam. In Germany, the brownshirts of Adolf Hitler smashed shop windows belonging to Jews, and 183 Nazis, duly elected by the German people, sat in the Reichstag and clamored for the power that would soon be theirs. The world was reeling through the blackest economic crisis in modern history. People everywhere were suffering from the ravages of unemployment—hungry, shabby, cold, angry, ill-housed. Their leaders, in this apocalyptic time, seemed unable to find a way through the storm. The world cried out for a new Moses.

In the United States in 1932, people were far too preoccupied with their own troubles to notice or care about the ominous rumblings abroad. Since the black morning of Thursday, October 29, 1929, when the stock market collapsed, sweeping away the savings and paper profits of millions of Americans and ushering in the worst depression in history, the nation had staggered, dazed and disbelieving, through its own *Kristalnacht* of deprivation, hunger, unemployment, bankruptcy, foreclosures, and despair.

At first, in the immediate aftermath of Black Thursday, the nation was undismayed. There was widespread confidence in the leaders of Wall Street, and the public believed that they would quickly fix everything and send the stock market spiraling back into the prosperity of the past ten years. The financiers themselves exuded confidence: they had reversed the downward trend of the market in 1907, and they would do it again. But in 1932, none of the fiscal wizards of Wall Street could think of a panacea and the economic scene grew blacker and blacker.

For a few months, the rest of the country was unaffected, or very little affected, by the crisis on Wall Street. The great corporations continued to operate at capacity, businesses went on as usual, and there was no notable drop in employment. But as the winter of 1929–30 settled in, and the stock market showed no signs of recovery, the other sectors of the economy began to show the alarming effects of the crash and the pinch of the Depression began to be felt everywhere. Unemployment rose, banks failed, small businesses went bankrupt, great industries slowed production drastically, and thousands of farms were sold at sheriffs' auctions. The Great Depression had settled like a gray fog on the land.

By 1932, twelve million men and women—a quarter of the nation's work force—were unemployed. Over a million men and boys wandered across the country scavenging and begging for food, with no destination in mind and little hope of finding a better world. They slept in the parks and doorways of the cities, and rode the rails or walked. "Unlike the traditional hobo," wrote William E. Leuchtenburg, "they sought not to evade work, but to find it."

They sought it in vain; there were no jobs to be found. Total wages paid out in 1932 were 60 per cent less than in 1929. The number of full-time workers at U. S. Steel had fallen from 225,000 in 1929 to none three years later, and the part-time force still employed was only half as large as in 1929. When the George H. Bowman department store in Cleveland offered 150 temporary jobs for Christmas, 1931, ten thousand applicants turned up.

Tarpaper slums, populated by the unemployed and the dispossessed, mushroomed on the outskirts of the cities and were derisively called "Hoovervilles," after the lonely, ineffective President. One Hooverville, in Manhattan's upper West Side, stretched for thirty-eight blocks along the Hudson River bank. The public blamed Herbert Hoover for the Depression, which was grossly unfair, since he had been in office just seven months when the stock market crashed, and the seeds of the Depression had been sown before he took office.

Steel plants operated at 12 per cent of capacity. Industrial construction plummeted from $949 million in 1929 to $74 million three years later. Many large projects, begun in the boom days—like New York's Empire State Building—opened their doors with three-quarters of their office space empty and unrented. Immigrant workers began to go back to their homelands: in one spring weekend in 1932, nearly four thousand left New York for Europe. America was no longer the land of opportunity; the torch in the hand of the Statue of Liberty seemed to have guttered out.

Even the schools were affected. In many communities, classes were slowed down to a three-day-a-week schedule, and the teachers accepted reduced salaries. Many teachers continued to work for nothing in cities where there was no money available, and there were reports of unpaid teachers fainting in their classrooms for lack of food. In Alabama so many public schools were forced to close that 81 per cent of the rural white children were deprived of their education for a time.

Outside the cities and towns, the situation was no less desperate. For lack of buyers, crops rotted in the fields, or moldered in storehouses. With food prices at an unprecedented low, tens of thousands of farmers went bankrupt, and the dismal crack of the auctioneer's gavel echoed across the country. On a single April day in 1932, William Leuchtenburg reported in *Franklin Roosevelt and the New Deal,* one fourth of the land in Mississippi changed hands at auctions. The farmers' response to the foreclosures was to riot. In angry groups of five hundred or more, they broke up the auctions of farms, or forced the autioneers to accept sales of a dollar or two, then returned the deeds to the former owners. The farm riots became such a serious problem in some states that three governors, Ben C. Ross of Idaho, Floyd Olson of North Dakota, and William Langer of Minnesota, prohibited any further foreclosures in their states to keep the peace.

It is remarkable that there was not more violence and rioting. There was a lot of talk about a revolution, though. "Right here in Mississippi, some people are about ready to lead a mob," shouted the rabble-rousing Governor Theodore Bilbo. "In fact, I'm getting a little pink myself." The Communists lost no time in infiltrating factories, farm granges and campuses, seeking—and finding—friends and recruits. But the communist threat was never very great, and the actual number of depression-bred Communists was always small.

Although the Communists were active, and the system of capitalism was undergoing a thorough reappraisal in the minds of many men, the mood of the average American was not revolutionary. There was, rather, a mix of apathy and hopelessness. The nation was ripe for the kind of totalitarian takeover which was then taking place in Germany, rather than a grassroots revolution of the people. And in 1932, there were plenty of home-grown Hitlers and Mussolinis in America who were eager to fill the political vacuum.

Herbert Hoover and his administration were adamantly opposed to any form of direct federal relief for the people. They were willing to aid the banks financially, but even the newly established Reconstruction Finance Corporation could not halt the metronomic failures of the nation's banks. Most of the few progressive proposals which the President presented to the Congress were turned down—frequently with the aid of callous Democratic congressmen who were willing to keep the country in misery in order to put the Hoover administration in ever-increasing bad odor, and thus insure a Democratic victory in the November elections. Relief funds, where they existed, were insufficient in most states. The breadlines and soup kitchens set up in large cities by municipal authorities and private charities were pathetically inadequate.

The official attitude toward welfare funds was that they were un-American, undemocratic and the harbingers of socialism. Even the American Federation of Labor was opposed to unemployment insurance. The British dole for the jobless was scorned and ridiculed in the American press. Proud Americans were supposed to take care of themselves; to accept aid from the government was humiliating, degrading, and dangerous. Yet, as more and more Americans felt the sting of poverty and hunger, that attitude began to change. The unemployed and the despairing looked to the men in Washington for relief that never came.

People were actually starving. One inhabitant of a Hooverville recalled that many of the homeless and jobless ate weeds. City garbage cans were regularly inspected by the hungry for edible refuse. Much of today's "Soul food"—dishes using the cheapest available foodstuffs—was concocted during the Depression. Even the city streets seemed empty. "Great numbers of people were sitting at home," wrote Frederick Lewis Allen, "trying to keep warm."

Along with its disaffection for the Republicans, the public began to change another of its deep-seated national attitudes, the awed reverence most Americans felt for the financial community. For a generation, the public had regarded the big money-men, the bankers and brokers, with the same hat-in-hand respect that English rustics once paid their earls and dukes. Indeed, if the United States could be said to have an aristocracy at the time, its seat was on Wall Street. Many leaders of the financial world responded in kind, and acted more like arrogant noblemen than merely the custodians of other people's money.

When Wall Street failed to stem the ruinous collapse of the market, public faith and reverence began to cool. By 1932, the stock market was the faintest whisper of its boom-years roar; the stock value of such prestigious giants of industry as General Motors had fallen from 72 and three quarters to 7 and five eighths, and U.S. Steel from 261 and three fourths to 21 and one fourth. Millions of investors were ruined in the space between those statistics.

Worse, some of the most respected leaders of the financial world turned out to be nothing more than common swindlers. A Senate investigation disclosed that a number of well-known multimillionaire financiers and corporation heads had paid no taxes whatsoever in the early years of the Depression, even though their incomes had continued at the six-figure levels of 1929. In March, 1932, Ivar Kreuger, the internationally famous "Swedish match king," committed suicide in Paris, and was revealed to be the forger of $100 million worth of bogus bonds. In the investigation of the wreckage of Kreuger's financial empire, Samuel Insull, the head of a vast network of sixty-five U.S. public utilities, was exposed as an embezzler, and fled to Greece to avoid imprisonment. The financial establishment, like the Republican Party, reached rock bottom in the public's esteem, and it would be many years (and after many federal regulations and restrictions had been imposed) before it regained a measure of the trust it had once enjoyed.

As the winter of 1931–32 warmed into spring, the nation and the world showed no signs of recovery; the national mood was as bleak as ever, and the future looked no more hopeful. "We could smell the depression in the air," recalled the critic, Harold Clurman. "It was like a raw wind; the very houses we lived in seemed to be shrinking, hopeless of real comfort."

In the spring, fifteen thousand angry, ragged "bonus marchers" arrived in Washington from all parts of the country, to demand extra compensation for their services in the armed forces during World War I. They settled in a verminous camp on the Anacostia River mud flats. While a few congressmen listened sympathetically to their pleas and demands, the government as a whole turned its back on them and acted as though they were not there. The city was hostile and fearful. President Hoover ignored the marchers, but acknowledged their presence in Washington by ordering chains for the White House gates and clearing the neighboring streets.

General Pelham Glassford, the harassed police commissioner of the capital, sympathized with the bonus marchers and tried in every way to alleviate their plight and to persuade them to go home, although he was opposed to the idea of a veterans' bonus. He managed to raise some money and stocks of free food from sympathetic Washingtonians. At one point, he arranged to have the Marine Band serenade the bonus marchers with such tunes as "Carry Me Back to Old Virginny" and "California, Here I Come," in the hope that the veterans would become homesick and leave. Since most of them had no homes to return to, the marchers did not budge.

The bonus marchers were angry and bitter, but they were always orderly and well organized. How long they might have remained peaceful is a large question. In July, after two months of uneasy coexistence with the veterans, Hoover was persuaded by his Secretary of War, Patrick J. Hurley, that the bonus movement was a dangerous revolutionary organization, inspired and led by Communists. It was true that there were a handful of known Communists among the marchers, but they were identified and kept in an isolated area of the camp. The overwhelming majority of the veterans were peaceful men, with no thought of violence or revolution. The President was convinced, nevertheless, that the bonus marchers were an ominous threat, and he ordered the Army to expel them from the city.

A bristling force, led by General Douglas MacArthur, had been alerted for months at Fort Myer, across the Potomac from Washington. There were four cavalry troops, brandishing bayonets and commanded by the flamboyant Colonel George Patton, a column of infantrymen, armed with tear-gas bombs, and six tanks. Within a few minutes of their arrival on the Anacostia River bank, they routed the marchers and burned their camp to the ground. One marcher was killed; the others fled through Maryland and Virginia.

The mood of the nation in its greatest crisis since the Civil War was sullen, fearful, and apathetic. There was no apathy, though, about one coming event. In 1932, a national election year, a new president would be chosen. In the previous three Presidential elections, the voters had selected

6

their leaders without much enthusiasm or interest. Now everything had changed. Interest in the 1932 election and the political conventions that preceded it was intense, for the voters fervently hoped to find a leader who would take them around the corner where, Herbert Hoover wistfully predicted, prosperity was waiting.

CHAPTER 2

THE REPUBLICAN DECADE

In the sixty-four years between the Civil War and the Depression, the American Presidency had been almost the exclusive perquisite of the Republican Party. Only two of the fifteen presidents in that time, Grover Cleveland and Woodrow Wilson, were Democrats, and Wilson, a minority winner, owed his first election to a disastrous split in the Republican ranks, when Theodore Roosevelt formed the schismatic Bull Moose Party and ran as its Presidential nominee.

It was a period, too, of almost unbroken conservatism, complacency and isolation from the affairs of the rest of the world. After the shattering experience of the Civil War, the young nation was in a mood for not rocking the ship of state. The United States was strong, vigorous, and prospering. There were, to be sure, some hideous facts of American life during those six decades—grinding poverty in the lower classes, brutal exploitation of the labor forces, vicious racial, religious, and ethnic prejudice, bigotry, disenfranchisement of most voters, ruthless warfare among the growing industrial giants—but most of the Republican administrations chose to ignore them. Only one Republican president of the period—Theodore Roosevelt—is ranked better than poor or mediocre by historians. Roosevelt was the only true reformer president of his time, and he came to the office of president only through the accident of William McKinley's assassination. The party's kingmakers regarded him as a loud-mouthed radical and would never have nominated him. Through all those years, the voters had been content to go along with a procession of lackluster chief executives and abide by a series of do-nothing administrations.

In 1920, the voting public had happily resumed its antebellum romance with the Republicans, but by the bleak year of 1932, the romance was over. Even some eminent Republicans had misgivings about the state of their party. "As an American," said Hiram Johnson of California, a towering figure in the Senate, "I have really shuddered at what four more years of Hoover may mean to this country."

It was almost certainly going to be a Democratic year. The Republicans hoped that something, some new panacea of Hoover's, some dramatic upturn in the country's fortunes, would set things right and keep them in power. But only the most Micawberish Republican really believed that it could happen. To most Americans it was apparent that any Democratic politician who was white and Protestant and had not been convicted of rape would almost certainly be the next president. The election seemed to be a sure thing for the Democrats, and, in the hindsight of history, it also seemed likely to be the last chance for democratic government in the United States.

Political connoisseurs would find it hard to match the three administrations that ruled the land between 1921 and 1933 for ineptitude, complacency, and weakness. They happened to be Republican administrations, but the losing tickets nominated by the Democrats were not much better. With the sole exception of Alfred E. Smith, the 1928 Democratic nominee, there was not a Presidential candidate of either party who was equal to the challenge of the office of chief executive in the 1920s. This, in itself, was not necessarily a disaster: inept, weak presidents had governed the country before (and have since) without leaving any serious scars. But the decade of the 1920s called for men of consummate political skill and clairvoyance, who could foresee and forestall the impending economic collapse. And, for all their good intentions, Warren Harding, Calvin Coolidge and Herbert Hoover had neither the vision nor the talent their constituents, the people of the United States, so urgently needed. To paraphrase an old Spanish proverb, the crimes were of the times, not of the presidents. But the presidents were not equal to the times.

Nineteen twenty marked the beginning of a Republican era that very nearly ended the Republican Party. After eight years of Woodrow Wilson's ventures into internationalism and the lacerating ordeal of the First World War, the nation longed for the placid, uncomplicated old days

9

under the carapace of isolationism. The notion of the United States as a leader and power in a corrupt world was repugnant to most voters. Wilson himself was a dying man, his dream of the League of Nations was widely believed to be a sinister European entanglement, and the Democratic Party was certainly unpopular, if not politically dead.

The leaderless Democrats met in San Francisco in the summer of 1920, and after long labor brought forth the ticket of James M. Cox, a Dayton, Ohio, newspaper publisher, and Franklin Delano Roosevelt, an attractive, ambitious young Hudson River squire who was virtually unknown (he had served for a time as Wilson's Assistant Secretary of the Navy), but whose magic surname was not. The Republicans picked an Ohio publisher, too, the handsome, amiable and totally incompetent Warren G. Harding, to carry their party's gonfalen. It should be noted, to the convention's credit, that Harding was not the popular choice of the delegates. He was actually selected by Massachusetts' autocratic, isolationist Senator Henry Cabot Lodge, Sr., and a gathering of party bosses in one of those notorious smoke-filled rooms, and railroaded through the convention. Lodge and his henchmen, most of whom were colleagues in the Senate, felt that Harding would be a "safe" president, whom they could trust to carry out their orders. He had spent four invisible years in the Senate, obediently voting as he was told to vote, and he would doubtless obey the bosses when he was in the White House. "How tragic for my husband," said Florence Harding, when she learned of the nomination, "and how tragic for the United States."

The Republican delegates must have felt something of Mrs. Harding's sense of foreboding, for they reacted angrily to Lodge's ruthless gaveling down of all protests and ramming the nomination through. In retaliation, they rebelled against the bosses and, at a time when Cabot Lodge was absent from the convention floor, named Calvin Coolidge, the dour Mayor of Boston and a political enemy of Senator Lodge, as their choice for the Vice-Presidency.

Neither party's ticket could be called brilliant by normal political standards, although the Cox-Roosevelt combination seems in retrospect to have offered a sharper, more promising choice to the electorate than the Harding-Coolidge ticket. Cox and Roosevelt campaigned vigorously across the nation carrying the old, outdated Wilsonian message. Harding did not bother to travel any farther than the front porch of his Marion, Ohio, home, yet he was overwhelmingly elected in November. For 1920 was a Republican year.

The Harding administration embarked, predictably, on a course of political toadyism, corruption, and drift, and ended on the shoals of the

Teapot Dome—the worst recorded scandal in the history of the United States government. With the sudden and mysterious death of Warren Harding, the icy, uncommunicative Calvin Coolidge took over the shaken administration.

The nation was shocked by the Teapot Dome—the deliberate sale and exploitation of governmental oil lands by ranking members of the Harding regime, which was either condoned or ignored by the President— and by the subsequent trials, imprisonments, and disgrace. As a consequence, 1924 should have been the year of a Democratic comeback. But the electorate soon forgets political scandals, and by 1924 the United States was in the midst of a giddy whirl of prosperity. There was no disposition on the part of the voters to change anything.

The Democrats muffed what chances they might have had by staging the longest, most frustrating and divisive convention in political history, and finally naming a candidate who was almost unknown. For three sweltering weeks and 101 exhausting ballots, the Democrats were deadlocked between Governor Alfred Emmanuel Smith of New York, the crusty, cigar-chewing beau ideal of the big-city masses, and William Gibbs McAdoo, son-in-law of Woodrow Wilson and custodian (or so he thought) of the Wilsonian tradition. The convention was stymied because of a rule, dating back to Martin Van Buren's day, that required a two-thirds majority vote of the delegations to nominate a candidate (the Republicans had long nominated their candidates by simple majority). Neither Smith nor McAdoo could muster the elusive 688 ballots that were required, and in their long and bitter battle in Madison Square Garden the Democratic Party was split cleanly into two factions and would not be fully rejoined for another decade. In the end, more out of exhaustion than anything else, the delegates named John W. Davis, a courtly and colorless Wall Street lawyer, as their compromise. Davis' only previous appearance in the public eye had been a fleeting, three-year tour as American Ambassador to the Court of St. James's (King George V had pronounced him a "perfect gentleman," but national politics in the 1920s was not a gentleman's game). Named as Davis' running mate was Charles C. Bryan, a rather dim politician from Nebraska whose chief claim on the Vice-Presidential nomination was, like Franklin Roosevelt before him, the fact that he happened to bear an illustrious name. He was the brother of William Jennings Bryan, the perennial presidential choice of the Democrats, but never of the nation.

The Democrats lost the election of 1924, along with any semblance of party unity, in the Battle of Madison Square Garden, and Coolidge, with Charles G. Dawes, a Chicago banker, as his running mate, won handily.

11

By 1928, national prosperity and the paper profiteering of Wall Street speculation was reaching into the ionosphere, and there seemed to be no reason why the United States could not become a nation of millionaires. There were plenty of reasons why, but hardly anyone noticed them. Calvin Coolidge, like Louis XV, may have foreseen the deluge soon to come, for, beneath his granite exterior, Coolidge had the instincts of a shrewd Yankee trader. In any case, in 1928 he "did not choose" to run again for another term. In his place, the Republicans nominated Herbert Clark Hoover, the cherubic millionaire mining engineer who had been Secretary of Commerce in the somnolent cabinets of Harding and Coolidge. The Vice-Presidential nominee was Charles Curtis of Kansas, an amiable but lackluster senator whose main political credentials were his proud claim to Indian blood (through a Choctaw grandmother) and a socially ambitious sister, Mrs. Dolly Gann. Hoover, with his starchy collar and prim manner, and Curtis, with his bumbling speeches and blinking bewilderment, were hardly the pair to stir the millions, but they were eminently satisfactory to Wall Street and to the Republican establishment.

The Democrats were getting into the habit of picking certain losers, and 1928 was no exception. Meeting in Houston, they managed to avoid the protracted warfare of 1924, and named Al Smith as their hopeful. Smith, one of the abler and more attractive politicians of his time, was nevertheless an insane choice for the Presidential nomination. He was a Roman Catholic —something to be mistrusted and feared in the primitive Protestant sections of the U.S. South and West—and no Catholic had ever before been elected president or even nominated for the highest office. A "Wringing Wet," he vigorously favored the repeal of the Eighteenth (Prohibition) Amendment, and this hurt him badly in those regions where drinking alcoholic beverages was regarded as a mortal sin. He was, moreover, the product of the Lower East Side slums of Manhattan—and therefore damned as the exemplar of all the corruption and evil of the big cities. Even Smith's famous brown derby and his jaunty cigar and twangy accent conspired against him everywhere but in the big cities.

As a sop to the South and the rural Midwest, the areas most fearful of Al Smith, the convention awarded the Vice-Presidential nomination to Joseph T. Robinson of Arkansas, leader of the Senate's Democratic minority. But Joe Robinson was not enough. Campaigning across the nation, Smith crashed head-on into a wall of bigotry and slander without precedent. There was talk of the Pope moving the Holy See to Washington, of Tammany bosses and monsignori running the White House, of the nation floating in legalized liquor. As Smith's campaign train raced across the South, flaming crosses, planted by the Ku Klux Klan, lined his route. And in November, the electorate handed Al Smith and the Democrats one of the most humiliating defeats in political history. Only five industrial states in the North gave their votes to the Democrats. Even New York, the home and heartland of Al Smith, voted against the embittered man who had campaigned as the "Happy Warrior." It would be more than thirty years before another Roman Catholic would make a try for the Presidency.

Herbert Hoover's triumph was brief: just seven months after he took office, the bottom fell out of the stock market and the grim Depression began. By 1930 the disenchanted electorate restored control of the House of Representatives to the Democrats, and dozens of Democratic politicians began to show the symptoms of Presidential fever. In 1932, the stage was set.

CHAPTER 3

THE
PRESIDENCIABLES

The Mexicans have a word, *presidenciable,* for a man who wants to be president but cannot say so in public until his political party meets in convention to select its candidate. In 1931 there were scores of Democratic *presidenciables* in the United States, but very few of them were candid or bold enough to come right out and admit their ambitions. Al Smith was one who played the coy game. The titular head of the Democratic Party, he had flatly announced, after the crushing defeat of 1928, "I have run for my last political office."

Two years later, in 1930, Smith seemed to be as far from the political scene as ever. He cited his financial reverses and his need to make money in private business as one reason for not going back into politics, and his religion as another. "There's no chance for a Catholic to be President," he told a reporter, "—not in my lifetime or yours."

The political currents had shifted, though, and Smith's closest political cronies urged him to reconsider. The prostrate country was crying out for a change of leadership—this had been proved emphatically in the 1930 Congressional elections—and 1932 loomed as the year of opportunity for the Democrats. By 1931 Smith was convinced that, even with his religion, his outspoken opposition to Prohibition, and his suspect city ways, he could win. He also felt that he was entitled to be president. The country owed it to him as compensation for the bad treatment he had been given three years before. He kept his ambitions to himself, though, and right up to the time of the Democratic Convention he convinced his closest associates that his only aim was to use any delegates pledged to him to swing the nomination to some other candidate—a candidate he never named.

Al Smith had another motive for running for the nomination without really appearing to. He wanted desperately to stop the candidacy of Franklin D. Roosevelt. This was a strange turn of political fortune, for Roosevelt had been one of Smith's strongest advocates in 1924 and 1928. In the marathon convention of 1924 it was Roosevelt who tottered out on crutches to the speaker's platform at Madison Square Garden and placed the name of Alfred Emmanuel Smith before the convention. It was Roosevelt who gave Smith the soubriquet that stuck with him for the rest of his political life—the "Happy Warrior." And it was Roosevelt again who nominated Smith—successfully this time—in Houston in 1928. For his part, Smith persuaded Roosevelt to run for the governorship of New York in 1928. Roosevelt had said that the crippling polio which had struck him down and left him virtually legless in 1923 was too much of a handicap and that any thought of reentering public life would have to be put off for years. But Smith, with a strong assist from Roosevelt's wife, Eleanor, convinced him that he could stand the rigors of a campaign and the pressures of high office. He argued that the Roosevelt name would be an asset to Smith's own campaign in New York. In the end Roosevelt agreed to run, although he was doubtful of his own physical stamina, and his own timetable did not call for a return to active politics until 1932.

The Smith-Roosevelt alliance ended with the elections of 1928. In the avalanche of bigotry and suspicion, Smith lost New York State by 100,000 votes, but the man he had pressured into running with him was elected governor by the narrow margin of 25,000 votes. Roosevelt's victory was a galling experience for the Happy Warrior—salt in the deep wound of being rejected by forty-three of the forty-eight states. After Governor Roosevelt moved to Albany the rift between the two men became much wider; Roosevelt decided to pursue his own political destinies without any help from Smith, and never once sought the advice or counsel of the older politician after taking office. Through the years, though, the two men maintained a punctiliously correct relationship, exchanging Christmas cards and birthday greetings, meeting occasionally at political gatherings and informal private lunches, but the warmth had gone from their relationship. In 1930, Roosevelt was reelected by a thumping majority of 220,000 votes and immediately raised his sights to the White House.

It was another embittering experience for Al Smith. Roosevelt had slighted him, had not sought his advice. Roosevelt was sitting at Smith's old desk in Albany. And now Roosevelt was going to reach for the job he had fought so hard for and lost. Sometime in 1931, when Roosevelt's intention to run for the highest office was quite clear to the least perceptive political observer, Smith determined to stop his erstwhile ally and protégé.

Al Smith, in his years of defeat and isolation, had changed. Although he still wore his rakish brown derby, pronounced "radio" with two d's, and remained the favorite of the city masses, he had become a different man. He was no longer the Happy Warrior, no longer the champion of the poor and oppressed. He had veered sharply to the conservative right. He was President of the Empire State Building Corporation, with elegant offices in that lofty tower. He served on the boards of banks and corporations. He had moved from the Lower East Side to a Fifth Avenue duplex. His friends were corporation presidents and Wall Street financiers. His political associates were millionaire conservatives like Bernard Baruch, the financier, and John J. Raskob, the legal counsel for the DuPont Corporation and chairman of the Democratic National Committee.* He had become, in everything but name, a Republican. (He took that ultimate step in 1936, when he "took a walk," away from the party that had made him a national figure, and cast his vote for the Republican, Alf Landon.) "He has ceased to be the wonder and glory of the East Side," wrote H. L. Mencken, a little sadly, "and becomes simply a minor figure of Park Avenue."

Roosevelt became a *presidenciable* when he first ran for public office in 1910, at the age of twenty-eight. He had been encouraged in his ambition through the years by his close friend, political cicerone and private secretary, Louis McHenry Howe. A frail and quirky little man, Howe abandoned a newspaper career in Albany to attach himself to Roosevelt and promote his political fortunes with a dogged fervor seldom equalled in American politics. After his tragic crippling by infantile paralysis, Roosevelt retired for a time to his home in Hyde Park and put his political ambitions aside. His mother, the hovering, domineering Sara Delano Roosevelt, urged him to forget about public affairs and accept the life of a Hudson River squire. But Howe,

---

* *Raskob, who had been a Republican in his youth, was Smith's own selection to be chairman, in 1928. Roosevelt had called Raskob "a bad choice" at the time, but since the presidential nominee has the privilege of naming the new national chairman, there was nothing he could do about it. The rift between Roosevelt and Smith began with the Raskob appointment.*

abetted by Eleanor Roosevelt and, later, Al Smith, insisted that he could and should resume his political career, crippled though he was.

Howe rekindled Roosevelt's ambitions by the crafty device of getting Eleanor Roosevelt to go into politics herself—first as a Democratic committeewoman, later as chairman of the New York Democratic Women's Committee. It was simple jealousy of his wife's political activities that finally persuaded the man in the wheelchair to resume his own career. By 1930, after his smashing reelection as governor, Roosevelt was ready for the big one. With Howe and James Aloysius Farley, the big, gladhanding chairman of the New York State Democratic Committee, he plotted a meticulous, thoroughgoing two-year program that is still the model of a superbly planned presidential campaign.

Roosevelt had many advantages as a candidate. He was a big, handsome man with a winning smile, a pleasant manner and a resonant voice. He was comfortably well-off financially, and well connected by family: Theodore Roosevelt was his wife's uncle and his own fifth cousin, and the name still carried great political prestige, whether it appeared under the Republican or Democratic aegis. Franklin Roosevelt's family had been members of the Hudson River squirearchy for generations. Roosevelt was a courageous man and a good administrator. His record as governor in Albany on public power, conservation, labor legislation, and unemployment relief had been liberal and forceful. He had an inquisitive mind, and his knowledge of the minutest political details was, as Fiorello LaGuardia put it, "aldermanic." His optimism and energy were boundless—his usual working day was fourteen hours. He was a proven winner at the polls, and politicians and voters, especially those of a liberal bent, were attracted to him.

Still, Roosevelt was no demigod, although many of his followers thought he was. A vain man who could be childishly petulant when frustrated, he had been raised as an only child by an indulgent, doting mother. (His elder half-brother, James, was a grown man when their father took Sara Delano as his second wife.) He hated to hurt people, and often pretended to agree with something he actually opposed rather than offend someone. This inability to state his true opinions gave him a reputation in some political circles as being shifty and changing his mind. He broke promises. He could be devious. With his political enemies and rivals, he was often ruthless and always unforgiving. He was theatrical, wearing a cape or a mourning armband on occasion, and brandishing a long cigarette holder. He was garrulous to such a degree that his wife always waited until mealtime, when his mouth was full, to tell him anything important that she wanted to say. His enemies accused him, with some justification, of weakness, opportunism, and vacillation.

Although his designs on the Presidency were well known to politicians all over the country, Roosevelt had to pretend he was not interested until the appropriate moment, early in 1932. At the convention of 1924, Roosevelt told John W. Davis that he, Davis, would be the ultimate nominee of that stagnant struggle. Davis was skeptical. "Maybe you will be the nominee," he said. "No," Roosevelt assured him, "my year will be 1932." He was right on both predictions.

John Nance Garner of Texas, the shrewd, cigar-chewing Speaker of the United States House of Representatives, was another leading Democrat with his eye on the White House. A former cowboy, and an able, professional political wheeler-dealer, he had a large and fanatical following that overflowed the borders of Texas into several Southern and Southwestern states. More importantly, he was admired by William Randolph Hearst, publisher of the nation's largest and most influential newspaper chain, and a political manipulator of considerable skill and experience. Hearst dispatched his star political writer, Arthur Brisbane, to Washington to question the little Speaker closely about his political views. When Garner's answers were brought to him, Hearst decided that he would back "Cactus Jack" as the man who came closest to representing the Hearst positions of fiscal conservatism and isolation from international entanglements. Hearst, who had once felt that he himself was destined to become president, despised Al Smith, who had opposed him many years before, and wrecked his budding political career. Hearst feared Newton D. Baker, the internationalist and leading advocate of American entry into the League of Nations. He suspected Roosevelt of internationalist and ultra-liberal convictions, and the other favorite sons were dismissed as inconsequential. So Hearst "discovered" Garner's candidacy and made him something more than a mere favorite son.

As Speaker of the House, Garner was efficient and well liked by Republicans as well as Democrats. An adroit politician, he knew the art of compromise, and under his leadership the House of Representatives functioned smoothly and efficiently. Garner's political views were conservative and pragmatic. A small man with white hair, owlish eyebrows and a cowboy squint, Garner still kept the early-to-bed, early-to-rise habits of his youth on the Texas range; he and his wife mingled in Washington society only to the extent that his official position required. And, although he was partial to cigars and Bourbon whiskey,* Garner was not, as John L. Lewis, the bombastic labor leader, claimed, "a cigar-smoking, whiskey-drinking, evil old man."

The likeliest of the dark horses was Newton Diehl Baker of Ohio, Woodrow Wilson's Secretary of War and the favorite of intellectuals of the nation who wanted to involve the United States in international affairs. A small, scholarly, gray-haired man with steel-rimmed glasses, Baker resembled his idol, Wilson. He was an impressive orator, and the country's leading advocate of United States entry into the League of Nations. His eloquent speech in support of the League at the 1924 Democratic convention had won Baker many admirers, but it had also won him the enduring enmity and suspicion of isolationists who did not want the United States to assert itself as a world power.

As the reform mayor of Cleveland at the turn of the century, Baker had pressed many progressive plans for municipal government into law, and he had the reputation of a hell-for-leather liberal. But Baker, like Al Smith, had become conservative. Fat years as one of the country's leading corporation lawyers, representing such gilt-edged clients as J. P. Morgan & Co. and the Van Sweringen interests, had changed his political philosophy. He sponsored a pamphlet urging the shutdown of a municipal electric power company he had backed when he was mayor of Cleveland.

Many ranking politicians, like Senator Carter Glass of Virginia, and influential journalists, like Walter Lippmann, liked Baker and urged him to run. At a Jefferson Day dinner in South Bend, Indiana, Cleveland's Mayor Ray Miller was cheered enthusiastically when he said,

> The Jeffersonian apostle of the North, the Presidential hope of those who are resolved . . . to return to the fundamental principles upon which the success of America has been predicated, the outstanding advocate of the God-given rights of man in America today is . . . Newton D. Baker of Ohio.

Baker was the coyest of the candidates in denying his interest in the Presidency. In June, 1931, he told a reporter, "As of now, it looks as if the front-runner is Franklin D. Roosevelt. I admire him and I hope he wins."

---

* *Garner and his Republican predecessor, Speaker Nicholas Longworth, established a hideaway in an office in the Capitol Building, with a well-stocked bar, which they called "The Board of Education." Every evening after the House recessed, they met there with their cronies to "strike a blow for liberty," and discuss politics. Over the years, many a legislative dispute was quietly settled in the convivial atmosphere of The Board of Education.*

But as the months marched on and presidential fever spread, Baker began to act as though he was more than mildly interested in his own candidacy. A handful of delegates in the South and in his own Ohio were committed to Baker, and many more had him in mind as their second choice for the presidential nomination. In March, just before embarking on a cruise to Mexico, he took the precaution of backing away from the unpopular League of Nations. His statement failed utterly to calm the fears and suspicions of the isolationists and infuriated Baker's internationalist supporters. Roosevelt made a similar disavowal of the League—which he had enthusiastically advocated as the Vice-Presidential candidate of 1920—a few weeks after Baker's statement, and was much more successful in shaking off the internationalist label.

By the time the Democratic convention met in Chicago, Newton Baker had active supporters in every state, and his presidential ambitions had grown to the point that he authorized the opening of a secret headquarters in the Congress Hotel, where his representatives could negotiate and bargain with delegates for their ballots.

If Newton Baker was the most invisible candidate, Governor Albert Cabell Ritchie of Maryland was the most forthright. When a reporter asked him, in October 1930, if he would like to be president, Ritchie answered instantly, "Of course I would. What man wouldn't?" The handsome, convivial Governor appeared to be the most promising of the favorite sons. His pleasant, photogenic good looks, his courtly manners and his record as a moderate governor all marked him as a political plus. Maryland's geographical location, between the North and the South, with no particular regional label, was another political advantage.

An outspoken advocate of states' rights, Ritchie had declared that the federal government was the most regimented in the world, after Russia and Italy. Politically, Ritchie was conservative enough to appeal to the Wall Street Democrats, yet not enough to scare liberal voters. He was meticulous in his public relations and was a favorite of journalists, many of whom he entertained at lavish terrapin dinners in Annapolis. He was the beau ideal of such Marylanders as Dean Acheson, Senator Millard Tydings, Henry Mencken and Gerald W. Johnson. During the First World War he had served as legal counsel on the War Industries Board, headed by Bernard Baruch. Baruch, the self-styled "Advisor to Presidents," was Ritchie's strongest supporter, although he made no public announcement of the fact and tried vainly to persuade other candidates that he was a neutral. Baruch had made the mistake, in 1912, of publicly endorsing Speaker Champ Clark for the Democratic nomination, only to see Clark lose at the convention. Baruch lost much of his own prestige and influence within the party as a result, and thereafter he always prudently refrained from openly backing a candidate until he was nominated.

John Raskob liked Ritchie, and Al Smith, who had long been friendly with him, recruited Ritchie early in his "Stop Roosevelt" movement. Ritchie was told that Smith had no personal presidential ambitions and would throw all the delegate support he could muster to some other candidate—who else but Albert Ritchie?—when the crucial balloting began. Ritchie was stunned and disappointed when he arrived at the convention and realized that Smith was definitely in the race for himself.

Another favorite son, and a strange one, was Governor William H. ("Alfalfa Bill") Murray of Oklahoma, the rustic, tobacco-chewing hero of the great plains. Alfalfa Bill, the darling of political cartoonists, seemed more like a character out of a hillbilly comedy than a serious contender for the nation's highest office, but his ambitions were just as sincere as those of any of the other aspirants, and under his cornhusker exterior, Murray was a shrewd politician and a man of considerable learning, who often quoted the classics in his speeches.

Murray had a drooping walrus moustache, and habitually wore unpressed pants under a dirty frock coat. He spoke atrocious English in the twang of the plains, but much of his outward appearance and manner, like much of Al Smith's, was an act. Politically, he was a progressive, a holdover from the Populist movement that had swept mid-America a generation before. When Oklahoma was still the Indian Territory, Murray was the attorney for the Chickasaw Nation. He served two terms in Congress after Oklahoma became a state, and spent ten years in Bolivia, accumulating a fortune in tin shares. As governor, he ruled Oklahoma like a Russian czar, and employed a bouncer to throw unwelcome guests out of the State House.

Hardly anyone looked on Murray as a serious candidate—except Alfalfa Bill. He hoped to be more than a favorite son, and tried to muster strong regional support from the Ozarks to the Sierras, but Franklin Roosevelt crushed his attempt in the North Dakota primary, and Murray arrived in Chicago with nothing more than Oklahoma's thirty-three votes, a kilted, all-girl band, and high hopes.

Governor Harry Flood Byrd of Virginia nursed presidential dreams of his own, and Smith could count on him to keep Virginia's twenty-six votes away from Roosevelt, for a few ballots at least. In Ohio, James M. Cox, the 1920 standard bearer, still hoped that lightning might strike twice.

In order not to offend either Cox or Baker, and to hold Ohio's delegation together as a bloc, Governor George White decided to run as a favorite son himself. Most political observers were convinced that White was simply acting as a front man for Baker and would turn Ohio's votes over to him when Baker emerged from the shadows. John W. Davis, the 1924 choice of the Democrats, was willing to run again, but with New Yorkers confronted with a choice between Roosevelt and Smith, his hopes were dim indeed. New Yorker Owen D. Young, the distinguished lawyer, corporation executive and part-time public servant, had many supporters in the conservative community, and, in spite of his earnest protests that he was not interested, Young was often mentioned as a strong alternative candidate if the convention again became a logjam. He was popular enough in some Southern states to be listed as second choice on the tally sheets of many delegates.

In Missouri, former Senator James Reed, a vain and ambitious man, was entirely agreeable to the suggestion that he might be a dandy deadlock-breaking candidate. He had been a powerful figure in Missouri as governor and senator, and in the 1928 convention he had been a favorite son and Al Smith's closest rival for the presidential nomination. Reed hoped to corner Missouri's thirty-six votes and attract the delegates of Smith, Garner and Murray after Roosevelt's candidacy was stopped by the anti-Roosevelt coalition. It was a wild hope, but Smith encouraged Reed, welcoming anyone with a delegate or two at his command to his resistance movement. Reed, at political loggerheads with Thomas Pendergast, the boss of Kansas City's political machine, could not command the full support of his own state's delegation, though, and Missouri sent a divided delegation to Chicago.

California's delegates, committeed to Garner after the state primary, were headed by William Gibbs McAdoo, the man who had fought Smith to the catastrophic convention deadlock in 1924. He was still Woodrow Wilson's son-in-law (although his wife was soon to divorce him) and presidential fever still lingered in his blood. The real commander of the Californians, however, was William Randolph Hearst, and when, at one critical point late in the convention, McAdoo suggested himself to Hearst as a compromise candidate, "the Chief" brusquely turned him down.

How McAdoo and Hearst could make common cause with Al Smith was hard to imagine. McAdoo's enmity toward Smith went back to 1924, when he had frustrated Smith in his bid for the nomination and precipitated the worst split in its ranks that the Democratic Party had ever experienced. Bad blood between Hearst and Smith went back to 1918, when Smith was a candidate for the gubernatorial nomination. Hearst, a resident of New York at the time and a man with burning political ambitions of his own, was also a candidate, and many of his supporters came to the state convention at Saratoga Springs. Smith won the nomination, however, and afterward the Hearst newspapers backed him in his successful campaign against Republican Governor Charles S. Whitman.

Any good feeling between the two men ended when Hearst attacked Smith in his papers for his failure to maintain high standards of purity in New York City's milk supply. Smith answered him in two public speeches, attacking the publisher personally. In 1922, Smith adamantly refused to accept Hearst on the ticket as a Senatorial candidate. The break between the two men was complete. Soon thereafter, Hearst moved to California. It is certain that Hearst and McAdoo would have opposed Smith, if they had thought of him as a serious candidate, more than they opposed Roosevelt, but they were willing to go along with him in the "Stop Roosevelt" coalition.

Illinois' fifty-eight-man delegation was headed by pompous old Senator James Hamilton ("Pink Whiskers") Lewis, a fixture in the Senate for many years, noted for his florid speeches, gaudy attire, toupee and sulphurous cigars. Lewis, a favorite son, was too knowledgeable a politician to entertain any dreams of the Presidency for himself, but there were advantages, he knew, to keeping the votes of Illinois in reserve for the highest bidder.

There was in the Illinois delegation an eager candidate with money to burn and a brazen yearning for the Presidency, even though he was virtually unknown and had no previous political experience. This remotest candidate of all was Melvin C. Traylor, the head of Chicago's First National Bank. Traylor was a close friend of Mayor Anton Cermak, the convention host, and he had fifteen or twenty delegates from the Chicago area ready to rally to him once Ham Lewis stepped aside. And Traylor had another hole card: he was an expatriate Texan, with Texas supporters he could count on if and when John Garner conceded defeat. After all, hardly anyone had ever heard of Davis or Harding or Cox or Coolidge before their parties glorified them with nominations. Of such stuff are political dreams and dark horses made.

These fifteen men, then, were the visible and not-so-visible candidates for the Democratic nomination. They represented every region of the United States and every political philosophy within the range of a democracy. And, among the 3,210 delegates and alternates who packed their bags and headed for Chicago in the final week of June 1932, there must have been hundreds of others who hoped that by some miracle they would become the fateful convention's choice. For there was very little doubt that the Democratic Party's choice would become the nation's choice in November, and the thirty-first President of the United States on the following fourth of March.

CHAPTER 4

BLUEPRINT
FOR A CAMPAIGN

In November 1930, James A. Farley issued a statement to the press:
"I do not see how Mr. Roosevelt can escape becoming the next presidential
nominee of his party, even if no one should raise a finger to bring it about."
This was in the rosy dawn of Roosevelt's reelection as Governor of New
York by the record-breaking margin of 220,000 votes. Farley's statement
was not impromptu, and Roosevelt's response was almost gleeful. "Whatever you said, Jim," he told his lieutenant in a telephone call, "is all right
with me." Thus began the penultimate round of a quest for power that had
been going on for more than twenty years. Roosevelt was off and running,
and thousands and thousands of fingers would be raised in his behalf.

The dream of himself in the White House had been cherished by
Roosevelt, certainly since the days when he entered politics as a young state
senator in Albany, and perhaps as long as the day when his fifth cousin,
President Theodore Roosevelt, was in the White House. The dream had
guttered out in the dark days after his polio attack, but had been rekindled
by the stubborn Louis Howe and by Eleanor Roosevelt. Now he was ready.
"For twenty years I had a perfectly natural and laudable ambition to become
President," Roosevelt told the London *Times*, "and was obliged to behave
like a man who wants to be President." In 1923, when he was still a young

man just past forty, he wrote a friend: "If I did not still have these crutches, I should throw my own hat into the ring [now]."

Howe had originally decided that 1936 would be "Franklin's year," but the specter of the Depression, the abject failure of the Hoover administration, and the size of Roosevelt's gubernatorial reelection victory caused him to alter the time schedule by one Presidential term.* He and Farley, with Eleanor Roosevelt, formed the cadre of the Roosevelt Presidential campaign organization. They were soon joined by Edward Flynn, political boss of The Bronx and an old Roosevelt friend. In November 1930, a few days after Roosevelt's reelection, Flynn was invited to Hyde Park to spend a night. When he arrived, Roosevelt told him, "Eddie, the reason I asked you to stay overnight is because I believe I can be nominated for the Presidency in 1932 on the Democratic ticket." Flynn agreed to join the organization.

Any compaign must have a liberal infusion of money if it is to be effective, and Roosevelt was not in a very propitious position: Wall Street's money men were largely Republican, and many wealthy Democrats were oriented more toward John Raskob (who had personally loaned the party $325,000 between 1927 and 1931) than to Roosevelt and the liberal wing of the party. But Roosevelt was an aristocrat, a member of the Hudson River landed gentry, and he had rich friends. Early in 1931, a "pre-convention committee" was recruited, to direct strategy and find financial support. These earliest birds to rally around Roosevelt were Jesse Straus, Joseph P. Kennedy, the Henry Morgenthaus, Sr. and Jr., all New York financiers, William H. Woodin, a disaffected Republican, Lawrence A. Steinhardt, Robert W. Bingham, publisher of the Louisville *Courier-Journal,* and Mayor Frank Walker of Detroit. The group later expanded as the Roosevelt movement gained momentum and took in such other men of substance and political clout as Joseph E. Davies, former Chairman of the National Democratic Committee and husband of the Post Toasties heiress, Marjorie Merriweather Post Davies; Homer Cummings, a leading Democrat in Connecticut and also a former Chairman of the National Democratic Committee, and Harry M. Durning, Governor of Kansas. All contributed money and fiscal advice (Woodin gave ten thousand dollars, the Morgenthaus, five thousand each) and all, or nearly all, were rewarded later with high governmental or diplomatic positions.

Howe was the grand schemer of the campaign. He has been described as Machiavellian, and he was. He had an instinct for where the power lay,

---

* *If Roosevelt and Howe had kept to their original plan, history might have been quite different, for Howe died in 1936 after a long, debilitating illness, and it took Roosevelt some time to find a substitute—Harry Hopkins—for the indispensable "Louie."*

and his dedication to "The Boss" was total—even to the exclusion of his own family. Howe lived at Hyde Park and at the Governor's Mansion in Albany, taking time off whenever he could to visit his wife and son in Westport Point, Massachusetts, from Saturday morning to Sunday afternoon. But as the campaign pace quickened, even these fleeting weekends became fewer and fewer.

Anyone who did not share Howe's complete dedication to Roosevelt and his cause was immediately suspect in the little man's mind, if not black-listed, and frequently subjected to violent tirades. And those who became too close to the Governor—Eleanor Roosevelt excepted—were subjected to a strange and unbalanced jealousy. Howe expected abject loyalty and at the same time a formal distance on the part of every Roosevelt adherent except himself. At the same time, he was the only person in the Roosevelt camp who could scold and talk down to "The Boss" and get away with it.

Howe was a strange man, nervous, rude, jealous, and overbearing, yet he could be pleasant when he wanted to. He was cunning and calculating, and a wizard when it came to campaign planning and political sleight-of-hand. A generation after Louis Howe had passed from the scene, Robert Kennedy, Lawrence O'Brien, and other aggressive campaign designers studied Howe's methods and maneuvers of 1930–32 and used them as a grand plan for the Presidential campaign of John F. Kennedy.

James Aloysius Farley, the third member of the Roosevelt campaign triumvirate, was Howe's diametric opposite: big, bald, nerveless, friendly. The son of Irish immigrants, he was—and is—a politician to the marrow. He had to go to work as a boy, after his father was killed by the kick of a horse. He was actively politicking as a teen-ager, and at nineteen, two years before he could vote for himself, he was elected postmaster of Grassy Point, New York, his native village, across the Hudson from the Roosevelts' seat at Hyde Park. Through the years, he climbed through the political labyrinth of Tammany Hall into state politics. As State Boxing Commissioner, he won the sobriquet, "Commissioner Cauliflower," and caused a sensation when he refused to permit the first Dempsey-Tunney heavyweight championship fight to be held in New York because Jack Dempsey had once refused to fight the Negro challenger, Harry Wills. By the time Roosevelt began his gubernatorial campaign in 1928, Farley was the State Democratic Chairman.

A pious Roman Catholic and a faithful marcher in the St. Patrick's Day parades, Farley attended every funeral, wake, banquet, and rally of any consequence in New York and joined every organization that beckoned. He flamboyantly signed all of his correspondence in green ink and although he appeared to be the most convivial of men, he neither drank nor smoked.

(His one vice: he was a chain gum-chewer.) His most valuable political asset, apart from his general geniality and friendliness, was an uncanny memory for faces and names. In his years of service to Roosevelt, Farley traveled to every byway in the nation, and his ability to summon up the name (and usually some flattering detail) of anyone he had met before became almost a political legend. Farley modestly downgraded the stories of his total recall: "Many a time I'd call out to a fellow and say, 'And how's the gentleman from Danbury?' and he would go away claiming I had remembered his name and address and the color of his wife's hair." Farley was an ideal choice to be Roosevelt's eyes, ears and legs in the political centers of the U. S.

Roosevelt realized that, in order to win national support in a divided country, he would have to present the faces of many different men in different parts of the country. To the South, he would have to be a moderate and a Wet, though not a torrential Wet. To the East, he would have to present an image of a reasonable Wet and a political moderate-to-liberal. And to the West, he would have to be the Lancelot of progressivism and conservation of natural resources, flying the banner of his own water-power and conservation legislation in New York state. It was devious politics, but Roosevelt, like many a Presidential candidate before and after him, was not above any deceptive masquerading as a practical path to 1600 Pennsylvania Avenue.

In the first months of his second term in Albany, Roosevelt had to pretend to keep his eyes modestly on the job at hand, governing the state of New York, when actually the lights burned late on the Hudson heights of Hyde Park and Albany as he plotted his course and studied the engrossing problem of how to become president of the United States. On January 29, 1931, Roosevelt piously wrote one Louis B. Fuglistaler of Vallejo, California, who had offered his services as a presidential campaign worker: "My time and energy are fully occupied by the duties of the Governorship, and although I am naturally gratified by the interest and support of those who believe me worthy of still higher office, I cannot concern myself just now with my own political future."

At that moment, Roosevelt, Howe, Farley, and the men around them were busily giving the body politic the most thorough examination it had ever undergone, down to the last pore and corpuscle of the smallest local precinct, with one thought alone: Governor Roosevelt's own political future and the smoothest means to elevate him to that still higher office. Howe traveled to Washington and sought out friendly political leaders, inviting them to come and talk to the man in Hyde Park. Farley collected the names of 141,000 precinct chairmen across the nation and had them transcribed on plates, so letters could be sent out and local intelligence collected on a regular basis. Roosevelt wrote a letter to each local chairman, asking for advice and a reading of the local political winds. Thousands and thousands wrote back, and a political army began to take shape. Newspaper clipping services were subscribed to, and the daily crop of newspaper reports was analyzed and condensed by friendly newspapermen. Roosevelt and his top aides were given their daily précis. At the peak of his campaign, Roosevelt's headquarters in New York received as many as five hundred clippings a day.

As the information flowed in, Howe assembled an enormous and very candid file of pink cards, listing all the available information on local political figures which might be useful. A sampling, from the file marked "Notes on Texans":

> JONES, JESSE H.
> Houston, Texas
> Money
> *Houston Chronicle* owner
> For himself first, last and all time
> Ambitious
> Promises everybody everything
> Double-crosser
> Fair relations with [State Chairmen] Sterling and Moody
>
> CARTER, AMON
> Fort Worth, Texas
> Non-committal
> Powerful
> King-maker type
> Loud
> Breaks with everyone
>
> CONNALLY, TOM
> Marlin, Texas
> U. S. Senator
> Politician—no convictions
> Friendly but non-committed
> *Tremendous* influence
> Key man
> Delegate-at-large
> Fears New York City situation [e.g., the impending investigation of scandals in the administration of Mayor James Walker]

FERGUSON, JIM
. . .
Support of FDR at early date could be *bad*
Support after commitment by Drys—O.K.

HOGG, MISS IMA
Very friendly
Money
Anxious to meet Gov. & Mrs. FDR.

Roosevelt meticulously answered every one of the letters that flowed into Albany from private citizens. The most trivial letters, even the crackpot mail, got polite, personal replies. A poem, urging his nomination and written in Italian, was gratefully acknowledged. Roosevelt was patient with panaceas: "Thank you very much for sending me the synopsis of your plan for social reform . . ." He carefully sidestepped sticky issues. When one M. W. Fry of San Francisco wrote, asking Roosevelt's position on the Massie case,* Roosevelt replied: "Naturally, at a time like this, whatever I do or say is subject to misrepresentation and distortion. I have been criticized for being too much of a fighter and not [being] aggressive enough, for saying too much and for saying too little, for being too radical or too conservative. . . ."

A campaign for a presidential nomination cannot be conducted by correspondence alone, but at this early, tiptoe stage, it would have been premature, politically rash, and physically difficult for Roosevelt to take to the road himself. And yet, he urgently needed personal liaison with the district leaders and local politicians. Eleanor Roosevelt did, as she had done ever since her husband became crippled, travel tirelessly around the country and report to him the reactions of the people she met. Louis Howe journeyed frequently to Washington to talk to national leaders and bring them back for an evening or a weekend of political scheming around the fireside at Hyde Park. But it fell to Jim Farley to be the candidate's principal advance man, drummer, and forward observer.

At first, Farley's excursions had to be discreet, under the cover of other business. The first, and most famous of his trips was in July 1931. A national convention of the Brotherhood of Elks was to be held in Portland, Oregon —and Farley was, of course, a Brother Elk in the bonds. With the conven-

* *The sensational trial in Hawaii of a U. S. Naval lieutenant, his mother-in-law, and two seamen for the murder of a Hawaiian, the alleged rapist of Lt. Massie's wife, Thalia. The four were freed, amid angry charges of racial discrimination, and the case churned up a wave of racial hostility in Hawaii and on the mainland.*

tion as a handy excuse, Farley and Roosevelt worked out a careful itinerary through eighteen states on the way to and from Portland. Farley saw eleven hundred Democrats, ostensibly talking to state chairmen about party affairs, but actually measuring the sentiment for Roosevelt. Each night he sent back a breathless report of the day's activities to Albany from his hotel room or Pullman berth. From Missouri, he wrote Louis Howe of an interview with former Senator James Reed: "I did not discuss candidates with Reed, but had a very pleasant visit with him. I think it would be a good plan to invite Senator Reed to visit Governor Roosevelt when he is in the East. I think he is a very vain character and he would feel quite elated by a visit with the Governor."

From Kansas he wrote: "As stated above, I road [sic] back from Topeka to Kansas City with Governor [Harry H.] Woodring, and he indicated very strongly that it was extremely essential that the Democrats nominate a Vice President from this section of the country, feeling that if we did, that we would absolutely cinch the farm belt."

Farley's optimism blossomed as he proceeded across the Western states. From Seattle, he wrote: "If I continue to find the same sentiment in the other states that I have found already I will probably reach New York so enthusiastic that I will make a statement and those who read it will believe I am a fit candidate for an insane asylum."

Farley was indeed overly enthusiastic, especially, as events later proved, about the big states of Illinois and California. But even in those important areas, he noticed certain signs that all was not well. From California he wrote: "There is, among a lot of voters, strong sentiment for Governor Smith, and more so than any other state in which I have travelled." He predicted, however, that California and Illinois would be in Roosevelt's pocket by convention time, and he was wrong. But in sixteen other states, his forecasts were remarkably accurate. It was Jim Farley's first sortie into the national political scene and a forecast of his future reputation as a peerless political prophet of convention ballots and, especially, of national electoral votes. Farley returned to Albany glowing with enthusiasm—an enthusiasm that infected the entire Roosevelt camp, except, of course, for Louis Howe, who was, as always, moodily skeptical.

The "Stop Roosevelt" campaign did not begin to gather momentum until the autumn of 1931, but there were occasional snipings at the man in Albany that presaged the struggle to come. Bernard Baruch remarked to the elder Henry Morgenthau, "Uncle Henry, if Frank is nominated, I won't give one cent to the Democratic Party." But, asked Morgenthau, hadn't Roosevelt been a good governor? "Yes," admitted Baruch, "but he's so wishy-washy." Baruch hastened to Albany to deny the story when it was repeated to Roosevelt (and also the charge that he had called Roosevelt "the Boy Scout governor of New York"). The Governor accepted Baruch's denial, but thereafter a frost settled on their relationship, even though Baruch did eventually contribute to the party and claimed Roosevelt among the eight presidents he had advised in his lifetime. (Actually, most of Baruch's advice during the Roosevelt years in Washington was given to the press from his well-publicized bench in Lafayette Park, across from the White House.)

More serious were the whispers that Roosevelt's physical and mental health made him unfit for the Presidency. Howe brought a report to the governor that Dudley Field Malone, the international lawyer, dabbler in politics and lifelong friend of the Roosevelt family, had called him a "cripple" and "mentally unfit" for the White House. Malone,* who was an outspoken admirer of Al Smith, was nonetheless outraged when the report filtered back to him. In a bitter letter to Howe, he wrote, "It is an absolute falsehood that I have ever to anybody at any time referred to Governor Roosevelt as a cripple, or made the least allusion of any kind to the fact that because of his physical condition he would not be able to stand the strain of the duties that devolve upon the President." To Roosevelt, he wrote, "I have and do seriously differ with you for personal and political reasons, but I am no gossip, and you know that my fighting is always done in the front yard, and not on the back stairs." Malone nevertheless joined Baruch on Roosevelt's "nix list."

The whispers about his handicap were the cause of genuine alarm to Roosevelt. From the time of his return to public life after his polio attack, he had striven to minimize his infirmity, recognizing it as the same kind of stigma as Al Smith's Roman Catholicism, something that could cripple him politically, if unfairly. It was true that his legs were virtually dead, and he could not walk without assistance. Every public appearance, where it was necessary for him to walk, either clinging to the arm of his son James or his bodyguard, Gus Gennerich, was an episode of physical and mental agony for him, and an example of his unquenchable courage.

From the knees up, though, the Governor was in robust health, and he felt that he had to prove it to the public. When he was running for re-election as governor, at the age of forty-eight, he qualified for a $500,000 life insurance policy, pooled among eighteen insurance companies, with the

---

* *Malone first registered on the public's conscience as Clarence Darrow's assistant attorney for the defense at the notorious Scopes "Monkey" trial in Tennessee. His final bow was many years later when, because of a striking physical resemblance, he played the role of Winston Churchill in the film,* Mission to Moscow.

Georgia Warm Springs Foundation* as beneficiary. The policy was widely publicized and quickly snuffed out the whispering campaign. Now, with rumors rising again, Roosevelt felt he had to prove his physical fitness once more. He thereupon summoned three eminent doctors to Hyde Park and submitted to a thoroughgoing physical examination over a three-day period. Their report, dated October 21, 1931, was glowing: "I wish to take this opportunity to congratulate you on the excellence of your physical condition," wrote Dr. Edgar W. Beckwith. "Your musculature is in a condition much above the average for your height of 6 feet 1 and ½ inches, your weight of 182 pounds is exactly normal, and that of a man who is in splendid health." Howe saw to it that the doctor's report got national circulation. The issue of Roosevelt's health did not arise again to any alarming degree until 1944, when he was indeed a sick man.

Through the summer, fall, and winter, Howe and Farley were busy keeping up with the deluge of letters and reports from all over the nation. In those days, long before computer systems, and with a totally inadequate, mostly volunteer, staff (the finance advisory committee had limited pre-primary expenses to a niggardly one hundred dollars a week, which was not enough to cover postage costs), they were hard put to absorb and catalogue all the incoming intelligence. But gradually, fragment by fragment, region by region, district by district, the national political picture began to clarify, and legions of Roosevelt supporters were recruited. The letters were mostly—but not entirely—encouraging to the Roosevelt forces:

From James C. Holloway, Austin, Texas—"Am sending you a list of the Democratic county chairmen from the 254 counties of Texas . . . Some people in Texas are trying to start a boom for Melvin Traylor, the Chicago banker, for President."

From Tennessee Chairwoman Bess Taylor Anthony—"Everything looks fine for our candidate in this part of the state. [Memphis Boss Edwin] Crump has given several statements saying he will actually support him. That settles Memphis! . . . The following is a set of the Tennessee organizations that have been approached by Senator [Kenneth R.] McKellar . . ."

Telegram from Howe to Roosevelt, in Warm Springs—"JUST BACK FROM WASHINGTON. EVERYBODY IN GOOD SPIRITS AND NO WEAKENING OF LINES [The state primaries in] ARIZONA AND WYOMING MONDAY AND WEST VIRGINIA TUESDAY SEEM PERFECTLY SAFE THE GANG SEND THEIR LOVE I WAS TAKEN TO THE CLEANERS AS USUAL GOOD LUCK."

---

* *The foundation was formed by Roosevelt for the benefit of the Georgia spa, where he went several times each year for treatment in the thermal baths, and where he died in 1945.*

In the autumn, the opposition to Roosevelt began to crystallize. Al Smith, in his Empire State Building headquarters, held frequent strategy meetings with Chairman Raskob, Jouett Shouse, Director of the Democratic Committee's Washington headquarters, Bernard Baruch, and other loyal sons of the Brown Derby. Governor Ritchie, Newton Baker, Representative Sam Rayburn of Texas (on behalf of Speaker Garner), and other hopefuls beat a path to the Empire State Building. Still others were approached by Shouse and Raskob and urged to gather in as many delegates as they could and hold the line for a nameless candidate who would eventually stop Roosevelt at the convention. The leaders of Tammany Hall were advised to line up as many delegates as they could as a threat to Roosevelt and a weapon for Jimmie Walker, whose corrupt administration by this time was under investigation and who would eventually have to be judged by Roosevelt himself.

As he learned of Roosevelt's progress, Al Smith grew increasingly bitter and angry, and his determination to stop his erstwhile friend stiffened. But, right down to the eve of the convention, he kept his personal ambitions secret. None of the other hopefuls in the "Stop Roosevelt" movement, and very few of his closest associates realized that Smith had been reinfected with presidential fever.

Smith's relations with the man in Albany continued to be correct— and remote. In November, he accepted an invitation to lunch at Roosevelt's Manhattan town house. The lunch was private, and the details were never made public, but the subject of the Presidential election was not mentioned once. Smith was a baffled and much angrier man when he left the lunch table. A few days later, Clark Howell, publisher of the *Atlanta Constitution,* interviewed Smith and sent off a lengthy letter describing the interview to Roosevelt, as Smith must have known he would do:

Dear Franklin,

I have just telegraphed you that I had a long conversation with "Alfred" this morning and that I would write you the details. You, of course, understood that I referred to Governor Smith. I had made an engagement with him at 10:30 this morning at his office in the Empire State. He seemed glad to see me. For a few minutes we indulged in generalities and then I got down to business, by telling him that my support of him "through thick and thin," and that Georgia's attitude toward him in the past, warranted me in having a perfectly frank talk with him. He replied that no man in the South had stood by him better than I had—that he was grateful, and that he would deal perfectly frankly with me.

I then said—"Governor, you hold in the palm of your hand the assurance of an overwhelming Democratic victory next year, or you are in a position where you could jeopardize the present prospect of such success."

"How?" said he—"By your attitude toward Franklin Roosevelt," I said. "With your support of him all opposition to him will vanish, and his nomination will be a mere formality. The country expects you to support him and it will not believe that you can possibly do otherwise."

"The hell I can't," he said—"but," continuing, "I do not mean that I will not support him. I am for the party first, above any man, and I will support the man who seems best for the party." I then went into detail to show him that no other possible candidate could give the party the same assurance of support as you could. "But you speak for the South," he said, and "you don't understand the situation up here as I do." I told him that you would get perhaps three-fourths of the electoral votes of the states west of the Mississippi. "But that is not this section," he said. "With your support it is," I said, adding, "You know that with Roosevelt as the nominee it means New York, Massachusetts, Rhode Island, Connecticut and New Jersey." He said he "doubted" it.

He then went on to say that "millions" of people in this section resented "the way he had been treated"—that "no Democrat had ever polled as many votes" as he had, etc.

"Governor," I then said, "is there any ground for personal hostility on your part against Roosevelt?" "No," he said—"socially we are friends. He has always been kind to me and my family, and has gone out of his way to be agreeable to us at the Mansion in Albany, but"—then he rose, stamped his foot, and said—"Do you know, by God, that he has never consulted me about a damn thing since he has been Governor? He has taken bad advice, and from sources not friendly to me. He has ignored me!" And then, with increased fervor, and slamming his fist on the table, he said—"By God, he invited me to his house before he recently went to Georgia, and did not even mention to me the subject of his candidacy."

I told him that you had been careful not to put yourself in the attitude of a candidate at this time, and I asked him if *he* had mentioned to you the subject of your candidacy. He said, "No"—that it was up to you to broach the subject, etc.

Then he got on the subject of prohibition, and became quite violent, indicating that you were "dodging." "Why in hell don't he speak out—he has been more outspoken on the subject than even I have been, and now ain't (it) time for trimming?" I asked him what he would do on this question. "Speak out," he said. "Speak what?" I replied.

"I would tell the country the time has come for a show-down against the iniquity of the 18th Amendment." "Do you think we should make an open campaign for the repeal of the amendment?" I asked. *"NO,"* but we should *"demand a referendum!"* I quite agreed with him as to the wisdom of that policy, stating that it was wise from every standpoint, and that such a declaration would receive the support of the drys as well as the wets—that I had, in the *Constitution,* warmly recommended Raskob's statement to that effect, and that while I had no authority to speak for you, that I felt you would support such a declaration. This seemed to please him, but he insisted it was too early now for committals, and that some of your "damn fool friends" here were at work organizing and arranging Roosevelt dinners, etc., and that they were doing you "more harm than good," etc. I told him that when he was a candidate his friends had gone much further, thus far in advance of the nomination than yours had now, and that thus far you had never said a word for the public as indicating your candidacy. "But the situation is different now," he said, though not indicating in what respect. He concluded by emphasizing that he was not for or against you—and that he was going to *take his time* before saying what he was going to do.

Roosevelt's relations with Smith continued to be proper and polite on the surface, but each man was keenly aware of what the other was doing, and each was too familiar with the perils of politics not to realize that they were on a collision course. At Christmas, they exchanged cards as usual. But with other party officials, Roosevelt was not so polite. After Jouett Shouse made a trip to Alabama, it was reported in the press that his purpose had been to get a "Stop Roosevelt" movement started. Shouse hastily wrote Roosevelt to assure him it wasn't so. From Warm Springs, where he had gone for another sojourn, Roosevelt sent him a reply that was biting, blunt, and, as far as his own political activity was concerned, deceitful—which Shouse certainly knew:

Enthusiastic friends of mine in different states have jumped to the conclusion that [while] you and John [Raskob] have very properly not come out in favor of any candidate for nomination next year, you are going to different states seeking to "block Roosevelt" by encouraging uninstructed delegations or favorite sons. They feel that this of course would be just as unethical as if you and John were to come out definitely for an individual and, of course, they are right in this point of view.

What many of them fail to realize is that I am taking absolutely no part in any movement in my behalf. I feel confident that just as Governor Smith is maintaining an absolutely correct attitude as titular leader of the party that it would not be correct for him to endorse any individual candidacy, so you and John will, as the directing officers of the National Committee, maintain the same position.

At the turn of the year the time for pretense ended and it became proper, in the best political tradition, for the candidates to declare themselves. And one by one they did. On New Year's Eve William Randolph Hearst, in a radio address, gave his imperial approval to John Garner. Roosevelt, Smith, Baker, and Owen D. Young were dismissed. "They are all good men in their way," Hearst declared, "but all internationalists." Cactus Jack Garner, on the other hand, was a conservative, thrifty cowboy, "another Champ Clark," who would ride to victory under the banner of "America First." Garner promptly agreed to run.

Early in January Albert Ritchie threw his hat in the ring, and Alfalfa Bill Murray entered the lists a few days later. Newton Baker never formally declared himself, but there was no doubt about his willingness and availability. Early in the year, perhaps out of habit, he advocated United States entry into the League of Nations, and then, twelve days later, he reversed himself and promised that he would not lead the country into the League until and unless a national referendum disclosed "an informed and convinced majority sentiment in favor of that action." Thus cleared with the isolationists (or so he thought), Baker began an undeclared, underground campaign and thought big thoughts about dark horses and second choices.

On January 28, two days before his fiftieth birthday, Roosevelt made his own candidacy official when he accepted an invitation to enter the North Dakota primary. "I willingly give my consent, with full appreciation of the honor that has been done me," he wrote. Two days later he received a warm birthday telegram, "HEARTY CONGRATULATIONS ON THE HALF CENTURY," signed Alfred E. Smith. There was no mention of Roosevelt's candidacy, however, and two weeks later, on February 13, Al Smith entered the contest himself, carefully mincing his words so as to reassure his allies in the "Stop-Roosevelt" campaign. "If the Democratic convention decides that it wants me to lead, I shall make the fight," he announced, "but I will not make a pre-convention fight to secure the support of delegates." Privately, he assured his allies that his candidacy was just a maneuver to win those primaries and nail down those Eastern delegations that were his for the asking. He told James Cox, though, that he thought he was entitled to the nomination.

CHAPTER 5

FIRST BLOOD: THE PRIMARIES

One of Roosevelt's first campaign innovations, after announcing his candidacy, was to form an advisory committee of intellectuals to write his speeches and help him arrive at positions on the issues confronting the nation. He needed to establish a national image, and quickly. The idea of gathering together a group of brainy experts was Roosevelt's own, even though he himself could not be called an intellectual. He read little, and got most of his ideas from conversations with others. Even so, he was a quick-witted man, and the notion of blotting up the theories of learned men appealed to him.

The committee was a political innovation that was to become a fixation in all future presidential campaigns. But if Roosevelt liked the idea of such a group, many of his advisors did not. Nothing like it had been tried before, and politicians usually felt uneasy in the groves of academe. Louis Howe was especially contemptuous of the committee, and it was he who gave it the name of "The Brains Trust"—later "Brain Trust."

To form his Brain Trust, Roosevelt turned to Samuel I. Rosenman, a brilliant young State Supreme Court justice and a close advisor. This may have been one reason for Howe's negative attitude: he frankly disliked Rosenman and resented his influence on Roosevelt. Perhaps as a sop to Howe, the first name Rosenman suggested was that of a young Barnard

College professor, Raymond Moley, whom Howe knew and liked. Moley, a specialist in politics and criminal law, was brought to Hyde Park, passed muster and became the Brain Trust's first recruit and recruiter.

Rexford Guy Tugwell, a young specialist in economics and agriculture who looked more like a matinee idol than a teacher at Columbia, was an early Brain Truster, along with Adolph A. Berle, Jr., whose field was credit and corporations. The fact that Berle was also doing research for Newton D. Baker did not bother Roosevelt; he was willing to share the young professor's talents. Other specialists joined the group as their expertise was needed (as many as twenty-five writers contributed to a single speech, Moley reported), but the cadre of the group consisted of Professors Moley, Tugwell, and Berle, along with Rosenman and Basil ("Doc") O'Connor, Roosevelt's law partner. Ernest K. Lindley, the *Newsweek* correspondent and author of Roosevelt's campaign biography, wrote one speech. Lindsay Rogers, a tariff specialist, was expelled from the group when he sent identical memoranda to Roosevelt and Smith, and the same phrase appeared, to the acute embarrassment of both men, in two speeches.

The existence of the professorial advisors was a closely-guarded secret for months. Howe was afraid that the newspapers might hear of the Brain Trust and make fun of it. He was even more fearful that Roosevelt's own name for the group, "The Privy Council" might leak out.

Each evening after classes, the professors journeyed to Albany, where they held lengthy after-dinner discussions with the Governor in the study of the Executive Mansion, returning to New York on the midnight train. Their existence was not revealed until September, when James Kieran, the Albany correspondent of *The New York Times,* overheard Howe make an unguarded reference to the group and ferreted out the story. As Howe had feared, the conservative press ridiculed the Brain Trust and categorized it as a cell of dangerous radicals. There can be no doubt, though, that the Brain Trust stimulated and enlightened Roosevelt, and wrote some of his most famous speeches. While presidents and politicians had relied on speechwriters, idea men, and kitchen cabinets for years, the academic, faculty-club flavor of the Brain Trust was a political novelty. Every subsequent candidate for the Presidency has had a similar group.

In addition to the Brain Trust and his financial advisory council, Roosevelt had a third force working for him—a group of lofty political confidants operating out of Washington and other political centers. Because he was most effective among the politically powerful, Louis Howe was assigned to the care and cultivation of these VIPs. He made many trips to

Washington, and a parade of senators and governors came, at Roosevelt's invitation and frequently at his expense, to Albany and Hyde Park.

As with the Brain Trust, the Washington advisory group included many men, but its nucleus was made up of three trusted allies, Senators Thomas J. Walsh of Montana, Cordell Hull of Tennessee, and Pat Harrison of Mississippi. During 1931, Roosevelt and Howe began a mammoth correspondence with political leaders—some five thousand of them—all over the country, seeking their solutions to national and regional problems. Months before he was an announced candidate, Roosevelt was arriving at conclusions, constructing the resolutions of the Democratic platform—*his* platform. Herbert Hoover, to be sure, was writing the Republican platform in the White House at the same time. But Hoover was a sitting President, and Roosevelt merely had a gleam in his eye.

In the spring, Governor Roosevelt sent Howe to Washington with a memorandum to Hull, Walsh, and Harrison, "a confidential interchange of tentative views relating to the platform, and not in any way to candidates." For fear of a press leak, the note was unsigned. The three Senators gathered together and produced an eight-point list of issues with their suggested solutions: Economic Reform, Agricultural Relief, Tariffs, Regulation of Public Utilities, Prohibition, Foreign Relations, Currency Reform and Unemployment Relief. Roosevelt sent the Senators' list, with some of his own emendations, to A. Mitchell Palmer, who had been Woodrow Wilson's Attorney General and was a gifted writer, and asked him to write a platform. He had some specific instructions, moreover: it was to be trim, succinct, no more than a quarter the length of the billowing, eight thousand-word platforms of the past. Weeks before the convention convened, Roosevelt had his streamlined, prepackaged list of pledges to the nation in his pocket. And when the convention's Resolutions Committee met in Chicago to draft a platform, the members, steered by Cordell Hull and stacked with Roosevelt's partisans, knew exactly where to look for guidance.

Never one to understimate the power of the press, Roosevelt nevertheless found himself in trouble in print even before he was off and running for the nomination. It was a situation that caused him much anguish. He had some newspaper support, including the influential Louisville *Courier-Journal* and the Atlanta *Constitution,* but most of the nation's periodicals were either flatly opposed to him or dubious about his qualifications. *Time* magazine was cool. The Republican New York *Herald-Tribune* was chilly, and the arch-Republican Chicago *Tribune* was downright glacial. Even among the syndicated columnists he found scant comfort. He could expect no support from conservatives like David Lawrence and Mark Sullivan.

Henry Mencken preferred Ritchie or Smith, and even such presumed liberals as Elmer Davis and Heywood Broun wrote scathing attacks on the man from Hyde Park. Broun's column, "Feather Duster Roosevelt, the Corkscrew Candidate," was gleefully reprinted by the Smith forces and distributed to delegates and the press at the Democratic convention.

The charges were the usual ones, ranging from shallowness, indecision, and vacillation through mental and physical unfitness to outright insanity and flaming communism. On January 8, 1932, two weeks before the announcement from Albany, Walter Lippmann, who was even then the gray eminence of American journalism, wrote a much-discussed column attacking the incipient candidate:

> Franklin Roosevelt is no crusader. He is an amiable man with many philanthropic impulses, but he is not the dangerous enemy of anything. He is too eager to please ... He is no tribune of the people. He is no enemy of entrenched privilege. He is a pleasant man who, without any important qualifications, would very much like to be President.

Liberty magazine featured a stinging denunciation of Roosevelt. The Scripps-Howard chain of twenty-five newspapers, which was second in circulation only to the Hearst syndicate, backed Newton Baker for a while, then suddenly changed course and endorsed Al Smith in a front-page editorial. "As Roosevelt generalizes, Smith is specific," it said. "As Roosevelt loves to delay, Smith loves action. Irresolution is ingrained in one, boldness in the other ... In Franklin D. Roosevelt we have another Hoover."

Beset and upset by the thunder from the press, Roosevelt began to announce his positions on the great issues. After the Hearst papers attacked him and insisted that he clarify his attitude toward the League of Nations, he took a strange stand at a meeting of the New York Grange, five days after announcing his candidacy. His disavowal of the League was sandwiched between two conflicting statements—a denunciation of the Smoot-Hawley Tariff Act, as a barrier to international trade (a peace offering to the internationalists) and a castigation of European nations for failure to pay their war debts to the United States (a bone for the Hearst isolationists to chew on). In the middle of the speech, Roosevelt admitted that he had been a leading spokesman for the League of Nations and for American participation in the League, but, he said, the world organization had not developed along the lines laid down by Woodrow Wilson, and "therefore I do not favor American participation."

It was an astonishing, inconsistent, weaseling speech, an attempt to please everyone. The press promptly denounced the speech as a cynical effort to shake off the Hearst attacks. Roosevelt's internationalist friends were deeply disturbed, and the isolationists were not impressed. The wonder of it was that Roosevelt managed to deliver the Grange speech with no damage to himself or his candidacy. His friends remained loyal, and a quick check of voting precincts around the country showed no weakening in the ranks of Roosevelt supporters, no signs of backing off.

Later in February, Roosevelt announced another stand, advocating the end of Prohibition and a return of liquor control to the states. The Wets were pleased (although Al Smith had no comment), and there were no signs that he had lost any support in the South and West. The speech, if anything, was a plus for Roosevelt, who was now making himself heard across the land.

On April 7, the candidate delivered the first speech which the Brain Trust had prepared for him. It was a ten-minute, nationwide radio address, sponsored by Lucky Strike cigarettes, dealing with "The Forgotten Man," and promising drastic social and economic reforms to help the jobless and the farmers of the nation. The speech had an electrifying effect. It was the first time that the entire nation had heard the hypnotic Roosevelt voice—a mellow, cultured, Groton-Harvard accented baritone that rang with courage and conviction. His voice was one of Roosevelt's most potent political weapons; it would comfort and reassure millions of people and infuriate political opponents in his radio "fireside chats" in the dark years ahead. (Many who disagreed with Roosevelt refused to listen to his radio addresses, saying that they preferred to judge them in the cold light of newsprint rather than fall under the lulling influence of the voice.)

The Forgotten Man speech frightened conservatives in both political parties. The *Wall Street Journal* called it "demagogic." Al Smith attacked Roosevelt and his speech and abandoned his nominal neutrality in a blistering riposte at a Jefferson Day dinner in Washington:

> I recently announced that while I would accept a nomination for the Presidency if it were tendered to me at the convention, that, until the convention assembled, I would not be for or against any candidate. I announce tonight an exception to that statement. I will take off my coat and fight to the end against any candidate who persists in any demagogic appeal to the working people of this country to destroy themselves by setting class against class, and rich against poor.

Smith's audience, heavily weighted with anti-Roosevelt coalitionists, gave him a roaring ovation. Roosevelt, alone among the leading Democrats of the nation, was not present at the dinner. Well aware that John Raskob had set a trap to embarrass him, he had sent his regrets at the last minute, pleading official business that kept him duty-bound to his desk in Albany. He had no public comment to make on Smith's angry speech, but his own subsequent speeches were notably more cautious in calling for flaming reforms.

Liberals, both Democratic and Republican, listened to the Forgotten Man speech* and to the other, more moderate and temperate speeches that followed it in the spring of 1932 and liked what they heard. Roosevelt's proposed program for combatting the depression seemed radical and fearsome to the business community, the incumbent Republicans, and the Smith-Raskob echelon of the Democratic Party, but to the average voter, feeling the pinch of the times, it seemed to be the only practical panacea in view. The Republicans and the conservative Democrats had no solutions, only vague promises that the crisis would pass.

The effect of the speeches was to make Roosevelt a rallying point for millions of disaffected American voters. Thousands of letters poured into Albany, Hyde Park, and the New York City headquarters Howe established in a cramped Madison Avenue office. Political leaders, especially in the Western states, liked the timbre of the speeches, and clamored to join the Roosevelt movement. Howe kept up a huge correspondence with leaders all over the country, and Farley traveled tirelessly through thirty-seven states to make personal contacts. Every weekend, and a dozen times during the week, the smiling Governor received important politicians who beat a path to his door. After a dinner in Albany, Senator Clarence Dill of Washington said, "I talked with him three hours, and came away a devoted and enthusiastic supporter."

"It was a closely knit thing," Farley recalls. "I did most of the running around. Howe was moody. He would not shake hands, so I got that job. He and I got along well, though, because he knew I was not trying to usurp any of his authority. He resented most of the others in the campaign."

Roosevelt had entered his name in a score of state primary elections, being careful always to steer clear of the private preserves of favorite sons. In other states, where the delegations to the convention were chosen by state conventions or by state committees, he worked closely with local officials, state committeemen, mayors, senators, governors, leaders of women's organizations, even newspaper editors. The heaviest concentration was al-

---

* *The speech even inspired a popular song,* "Remember Your Forgotten Man," *in the Hollywood musical,* Gold Diggers of 1933.

ways on those states where the delegates were "instructed," or pledged to vote for a specific candidate, or where the "unit rule" prevailed, and delegates were bound to cast the entire delegation's vote for the candidate favored by the majority. Before the primaries, Roosevelt put all the pressure at his command on those states where he held an apparent majority of the delegates to accept the unit rule, thereby binding the entire delegation to his candidacy. Mrs. Isabella Greenway, chairman of the Arizona delegation, was opposed to instructed delegations, but she was also a lifelong friend of the Roosevelts (she had been one of Eleanor Roosevelt's bridesmaids), and she eventually agreed to the request from Hyde Park. The Arizonans came to Chicago pledged to vote for Roosevelt. In other states, where Roosevelt supporters were in the minority, the shoe was on the other foot, and Howe and Farley lobbied grimly for uninstructed delegations.

In some states and large cities, where political machines controlled the selection of delegates, it was necessary to deal with just one man, the local boss. Thus, when Senator Burton Wheeler brought Huey Long to Albany and persuaded him to join the Roosevelt cause, Roosevelt could count on the ballots of the Louisiana delegation, for Long did not even bother to call the full state Democratic Committee together when he personally selected the members of the delegation. "We vote as a unit on everything," Huey Long explained with a straight face. Similarly, Kansas City Boss Pendergast was able to deliver half the Missouri delegation, after a friendly visit from Farley and some friendlier correspondence from Albany. In his preconvention campaign, Roosevelt always worked at the state and local level, never on a nationwide scale, which was a prudent policy, inasmuch as he would have had to deal with the Democratic National Committee in order to launch a national campaign, and the National Committee was directed by his sworn enemies.

The Democratic National Committee nominally controls the machinery of the political convention—membership of the various committees, names of the chairmen, the keynote speaker, and so on—but the master machinist, in both parties, is usually one man, who manipulates the national committee and dictates its choices—an incumbent President, or the candidate with the greatest preconvention delegate power. In 1932, Roosevelt was determined to dominate the national committee, despite Raskob and Shouse, and to put his own partisans in all the key positions. Long before the national committee met, Howe had written each state delegation chairman or the local Roosevelt spokesman, in states where the chairmen were unfriendly, asking for a list of delegates for each convention committee.

Soon, tangible currency for his campaign—delegate support for the convention—began to accumulate in Roosevelt's corner. In New Hampshire, the first primary, Roosevelt defeated Smith. In the South and in the border states, where primary elections were a rarity, Roosevelt accumulated twelve out of sixteen delegations. Mississippi accredited a restive delegation which was committed to cast its twenty votes for Roosevelt under the unit rule, by the slim margin of one vote and the continuous pressure brought by Pat Harrison. In Georgia, John Garner, with the shrill support of Hearst's Atlanta *Journal,* rashly challenged the man from Albany in the primary election and was crushed by a margin of eight to one. Roosevelt was especially pleased by the result in Warm Springs, where the voters turned out to support him 218 to one. In Kentucky, some diligent negotiations by Barry Bingham, Joseph Guffey of Pennsylvania, and Farley persuaded Alben Barkley, a pudgy young senator, to give up his ambition to run as a favorite son, and swung the state behind Roosevelt. Harry Byrd at first gave Roosevelt a vague promise that he could have Virginia's votes. He opposed many of the liberal fiscal policies emanating from Albany, but he and his famous brother, Admiral Richard E. Byrd, were close friends of the Roosevelt family. Later, Byrd decided to make a serious run for the nomination himself, as Virginia's favorite son. He hinted that he would swing his ballots to Roosevelt when his own candidacy seemed hopeless. South Carolina fielded an uninstructed delegation, but Senator James Byrnes privately assured Roosevelt that the votes were his. On May 23, Howe received a proud telegram from Nashville: "TENNESSEE CONVENTION TODAY UNANIMOUSLY INSTRUCTED ITS DELEGATION FOR GOVERNOR ROOSEVELT."

In the state primaries, Roosevelt's showing was excellent—at first. He won impressively in Alaska, Washington, North Dakota, Iowa, Maine, and Wisconsin. These were all sparsely populated areas, with a relatively low harvest of votes. In the big, densely populated states of the East, Midwest, and California, Roosevelt's luck was not so good. He was persuaded to enter the Massachusetts primary by his eldest son, James, a young Boston insurance agent, recently graduated from Harvard, and by James Michael Curley, the conniving, maverick ex-Mayor of Boston. It was a reckless move, for the name of Al Smith had been entered in the Bay State primary, and Smith was still a hero of the large urban population there. Curley, moreover, was anathema to the leaders of Massachusetts' political machine, Governor Joseph B. Ely and Senator David I. Walsh.* A terse note from Massachusetts State Democratic Chairman Frank Donohue warned Howe of

* *No relation to Senator Thomas Walsh of Montana.*

trouble ahead. "This delegation is for Alfred E. Smith," Donohue wrote. "Aside from that, it is against no other candidate." In an effort to head off trouble, Roosevelt arranged a meeting of Ely, Walsh, Senator Marcus Coolidge, Curley, and Colonel Edward House, Woodrow Wilson's political impresario, at House's summer home in Manchester-by-the-Sea, Massachusetts. The conferees were making progress toward some sort of face-saving deal when they received word that Curley had chosen that day to deliver a venomous speech denouncing Smith as a spoiler and announcing his own support of Roosevelt. Negotiations ended on the spot, and Roosevelt lost the primary to Smith in a landslide. As a footnote to the primary, Curley was unable to win a place for himself in the Massachusetts delegation, but managed to get to the convention as a delegate from Porto Rico.*

Roosevelt was unable to claim his own state, with its ninety-six votes. New York's mission to the convention was made up of delegates-at-large, chosen by the State Democratic Committee, and locally elected district delegates. On the advice of Smith and Raskob, the Tammany Hall representatives on the state committee chose delegates-at-large from their own ranks and sent them to Chicago uninstructed. This was a political threat, designed to save Jimmie Walker, New York City's corruption-tainted mayor who by that time was facing dismissal on charges of malfeasance and misappropriation of the city's funds. If Roosevelt fired Walker, the Tammany votes would go to Smith; if he left Walker in office, the votes might be cast for him. The district delegates were split evenly between Smith and Roosevelt. The result was that Governor Roosevelt commanded fewer than half the votes from New York.

Mayor Frank Walker of Detroit and G. Hall Roosevelt, the city's comptroller and brother of Eleanor Roosevelt, succeeded in swinging Michigan's big delegation behind Roosevelt, but Michigan provided almost the only cheering note from the Midwest. Indiana's delegation, led by handsome Paul McNutt, a World War I hero and candidate for governor, was up for grabs. Publisher Roy Howard, still backing Newton D. Baker, offered McNutt the endorsement of the Scripps-Howard newspaper chain for his state ticket in exchange for eight Indiana votes for Baker in the first three ballots. In neighboring Illinois, the delegation was controlled by Mayor Cermak, who was a friend of Melvin Traylor, but inclined to listen to the siren song of Al Smith and the anti-Roosevelt establishment. Farley went to Chicago, bearing prestigious and powerful convention jobs as a lure, but

---

* *The island territory's original Spanish name, Puerto Rico, was formally restored to it in 1933.*

Cermak eventually decided to play a waiting game and lined up Illinois' fifty-eight votes behind Ham Lewis, to be held in reserve.

In the Pennsylvania primary, Smith got a sizable and surprising vote and claimed nearly half of the state's divided delegation. Connecticut, bound to vote unanimously under the unit rule, Rhode Island, and New Jersey were all Al Smith's for the asking.

In Ohio, after much rosy correspondence and negotiation with Governor White, Howe had reason to believe the state would swing behind his candidate. But the Governor was courted just as vigorously by Raskob, Smith, and James Cox, and he finally announced that he would run himself, as a favorite son. He justified his switch to Howe by saying he did not want to give offense to Cox or Baker, both Ohioans and both presidential possibilities. Colonel C. W. Durban, former chairman of the Ohio Democratic Committee, angrily wrote Howe that White had sold out to the anti-Roosevelt forces. "Democrats of Ohio were astounded to find Governor George White in alliance with the 'Stop Roosevelt' movement," he wrote Howe. "When the people of Ohio discover this, they will quickly call Governor White to account."

After his initial successes in the Southern and Mountain states, Roosevelt was frustrated in state after powerful state from the New England littoral to the Mississippi River. The hardest blow, though, was yet to come. There seemed to be no reason to believe that California would not flock to the Roosevelt standard along with the neighboring Western states. But California is different. California is unpredictable. California had given the Presidency to Woodrow Wilson.* And California, in 1932, denied Roosevelt the primary votes that would have locked up the nomination for him.

It was a furious three-way contest between Smith, Roosevelt, and Garner. The state seemed safe for Roosevelt until Smith, flushed with his victory in Massachusetts, entered the race. McAdoo rushed to support Garner, and there were many other partisans of the crusty little Speaker among the large population of transplanted Texans who had moved to Southern California. The huge Texas-California Association helped Garner's

---

* *Many political historians believe that California voted for Woodrow Wilson in 1916 because Charles Evans Hughes, the Republican candidate, neglected to call on Hiram Johnson, long the leading Republican and king-maker in California, when both men were staying at the same hotel. Johnson's, and California's, fury at the slight may have turned the tide to Wilson in the famous morning-after election when Hughes went to bed certain that he was President-elect, and woke up to find that he had lost California and the election. Roosevelt made no such gaffe. When he got to California, he made a point of paying his respects to the venerable Johnson, charmed him, and won his tacit support.*

campaign, but the most substantial backing came from William Randolph Hearst, who ordered an all-out editorial campaign, hailing the Texan as a new Moses and damning his eastern rivals in the blackest terms short of libel. What had failed in Georgia apparently worked in California, for Garner won the primary easily, with 216,000 votes, to 170,000 for Roosevelt, and 138,000 for Smith. John Garner's candidacy instantly rose from regional to national stature, and Roosevelt came to the painful realization that he would have to face an all-out struggle for delegates in Chicago. If he had succeeded in cornering California's forty-four votes, his preconvention tally would have been too close to the two-thirds majority mark to deny him the nomination. Now, with the last of the big primaries behind him, he had to face a bitter fight.

From his bastion in San Simeon, Hearst gloated over his triumph. Arthur Brisbane let the world know about it through his newspaper column: "Speaker Garner seems to have won the California primaries, defeating Governor Roosevelt and former Governor Smith. This does not surprise those who know that the five powerful newspapers owned by Mr. Hearst in California have all supported Mr. Garner." McAdoo was jubilant. "It seems a serious and perhaps irreparable blow to the Roosevelt candidacy," he crowed.

The "Stop Roosevelt" group continued its search for a standard bearer who could unite the favorite sons. Smith and Raskob approached Owen D. Young, and he bluntly refused the honor. Newton D. Baker also refused, though not so emphatically. Raskob promoted Melvin Traylor in Texas and Kentucky, with faint hopes and fainter responses. Governor Ritchie came to New York for a conference with Raskob and Smith, and Bernard Baruch praised him at a banquet, then traveled to Albany to assure Roosevelt that he was not really backing any single candidate.

Raskob traveled through the South, talking endlessly about the need to repeal the Prohibition Act and praising Newton Baker. Shouse spoke to district leaders in the Midwest and South, urging them to send uninstructed delegations to the convention. The campaign of character assassination went on. "We don't want a dead man in the White House," McAdoo told Dan Roper, an old friend, but also an active lieutenant in Roosevelt's camp. If Roosevelt won the election, McAdoo told Bruce Kremer, another Roosevelt partisan, he would "Tammanyize the federal government."

Without a beau ideal or a cause to rally around, the anti-Roosevelt coalition became an essentially negative movement. Its active leaders—Smith, Raskob, Shouse, Ely, Mayor Frank Hague of Jersey City—actually wanted just one candidate, Al Smith, to lead their movement and wrest the nomination from Roosevelt, but Smith was the one candidate who was unacceptable to the others.

With all of his opponents, especially the favorite sons, Roosevelt maintained a courteous, tactful relationship. With Speaker Garner, his relations were quite cordial. Garner asked Howe to tell him where Roosevelt stood on a number of national issues that would be discussed at a caucus of House Democrats. He wanted, as a courtesy, to let the Congressmen know how the Governor of New York felt. The one candidate who caused the most uneasiness in Albany was the shadowy Baker. Through the spring, Farley constantly canvassed and recanvassed his correspondents and district leaders in the South to determine how much support Baker was getting.

As his campaign gathered momentum, Roosevelt attracted some strange supporters, but at that point in his political career he did not examine the credentials of his followers too closely, and all were welcome. Some, like the ranting Huey Long, were difficult to keep in line, but very helpful in backroom deals. Father Charles Coughlin, the notorious "radio priest" of Detroit's Church of the Little Flower, helped bring Michigan into the Roosevelt camp. Roosevelt put considerable trust—too much, in the opinion of some of his advisors—in Boss Pendergast of Kansas City. Roosevelt sought unsuccessfully to bring the convention to Kansas City, which he felt would be friendlier to him than Chicago. His dalliance with Pendergast was certain to offend James Reed and to violate his policy of not stepping on the toes of favorite sons. It sent Reed running to the camp of Al Smith, and was of dubious value to the Roosevelt cause. James Michael Curley was a real liability in the Massachusetts debacle, but he was helpful later in the campaign in dealing with Hearst.

In placing so much faith in Colonel House, Roosevelt made another error in judgment. The Colonel had indeed been a man of political influence in the far-away days of Woodrow Wilson, and the impression he had made on Franklin Roosevelt as a youthful Assistant Secretary of the Navy had lingered on. Louis Howe had great faith in House, too, and he urged Roosevelt to give House an important role in the campaign. But House's influence had died with Wilson, his skill at wheeling and dealing had been spent on an older political generation. House presided over the disastrous meeting in Massachusetts, and he had several conversations with Hearst, assuring him that Roosevelt was actually a very conservative man, with no desire to dabble in international affairs. Hearst demanded that Roosevelt disengage himself from his League of Nations position as proof. House reported the demand to Albany, and Roosevelt obediently complied, in his speech to the New York Grange, only to receive a savage drubbing in the Hearst press during the California primary. Some observers on the Roosevelt campaign staff blamed Colonel House for the loss of Texas and California.

As the winter–spring campaign intensified, Roosevelt's need for funds increased. A budget of ninety thousand dollars was projected for the first three months, and wealthy supporters like Joseph P. Kennedy, the Morgenthaus, and New York's Lieutenant Governor Herbert Lehman, willingly provided it, but it was still not enough. In his cluttered, windowless office at the Madison Avenue headquarters, Louis Howe was hard-put to pay all the bills. The staff grew to six hundred workers, and although most of them were volunteers, the campaign payroll rose to $26,000 a week. The cost of mailing what would eventually exceed 63 million pieces of campaign literature, five million buttons, and three million personally addressed letters was enormous. Threatening letters arrived with every mail. The lawyer for the Bobbs-Merrill publishing company, demanding payment of $280.45, wrote, "I shall withhold filing suit until Saturday . . ." An Atlantic City boardwalk painter who had sketched a portrait of Roosevelt which he used on a campaign brochure wrote a plaintive note: "You probably have overlooked in sending [sic] the check that you mentioned in the last letter. Artists, too, sometimes become materialists in order to live. May I be favored?" Western Union was telegraphic in its demand: "ATTENTION PAST DUE ACCOUNT REQUESTED. PLEASE REMIT TODAY. CREDIT MANAGER." And Luce's clipping bureau, asking for payment for four months service, demanded: "PAST DUE—PAST DUE. PLEASE REMIT."

There were other expenses. Joe Guffey submitted an expense account for $87.50 for a trip to Kentucky which, if it was the price of persuading Alben Barkley to take his delegation into the Roosevelt fold, was the biggest geopolitical bargain since the purchase of Manhattan Island. The faithful had to be transported to and from Albany for strategy meetings. A telegram of the time, to a group of eight key advisors from Washington, read: "PLEASE GO TO TICKET WINDOW THREE GRAND CENTRAL STATION AND YOU WILL FIND AN ENVELOPE WITH YOUR TICKET AND PARLOR CAR SEAT. THE RAILROAD IS GIVING US A CAR SO THAT WE CAN TALK ON THE WAY UP. TRAIN LEAVES NEW YORK EIGHT THIRTY DAYLIGHT SUNDAY MORNING. LOUIS MC HENRY HOWE." In this instance, the transportation may have been gratis, since Cornelius Vanderbilt, Jr., grandson of the founder of the New York Central Railroad was a close friend and supporter of Governor Roosevelt and had, in fact, accepted the post of doorman at Roosevelt's Chicago headquarters. (He proved to be a very inept doorman at the convention, though, refusing to admit Herbert Lehman on one occasion, because he did not recognize the lieutenant governor.)

As the convention date drew near, Howe, Farley, and Roosevelt busied themselves with last-minute plans. Howe refused to delegate any authority—even down to such minutiae as authorizing the installation of two water coolers at the Congress Hotel headquarters. He and Roosevelt debated the merits of blue-and-white bunting (at a rental price of $175) over sateen ($20 more), and decided to shoot the works on sateen. One conference room at the headquarters, which might have been called an early-day VIP Lounge, was set aside for the *autos da fé* of hesitant delegates. There, on Howe's insistence, a direct telephone line was linked up between the Governor's study in Albany and an amplifying system in the room. It cost $630.20 for three days and $206.40 for each additional day, and it was worth every penny. After the convention got under way, groups of dubious delegates would be shepherded into the Orwellian chamber, and the famous voice would flood the room to inspire and enfold them: "My friends from Missouri . . ." followed by carefully-coached personal references, first names, and gentle answers to hard questions. There is no doubt that many a delegate who entered the room a skeptic emerged a devoted convert. The Fireside Chat had been born.

Howe was just as thoroughgoing in his preparations at the Chicago Stadium. Three adjoining, highly secret rooms on the gallery floor were set aside, after the payment of a bribe to stadium attendants, for Farley's off-the-floor conferences. The central room was to be used for meetings, and the two flanking rooms were to be locked and empty, to keep eavesdroppers at bay. Howe further insisted that a staff worker be assigned to sleep in the inner sanctum for a week before the convention, to keep squatters and listening devices out. The suspicious old man even refused to employ local telephone operators at the headquarters, for fear of a leak, assigning instead Louise ("Hacky") Hachmeister, the chief operator in Albany, with a team of trusted operators, to man the switchboard. To guard his own secluded suite at the Congress, No. 1702, Howe chose his own son, Hartley, and his secretary, Lela ("Rabbit") Stiles* to be doormen.

A folding vest-pocket directory, with a map of the Congress Hotel and a list of the state delegations, their locations and telephone numbers, was printed and issued to staff members, very important politicians, and the press. Howe was almost fanatical about keeping lists of everything and anything related to the campaign. He had a list of state committeewomen, a list of people to be given seats in the galleries (New York was allotted just 700

---

* *The Roosevelt ménage was much given to cute nicknames. Margaret Lehand, Roosevelt's secretary, was "Missy," and Roosevelt and Rosenman were called, behind their backs, "Franklin the Roose" and "Sammy the Rose."*

of the 18,420 seats available, and the lion's share of these went to Tammany Hall), lists of delegates, with different colored tabs to distinguish among regulars, alternates and delegates-at-large. One list was headed, "Those we have relied on to conduct the fight for delegates in the different states."

A note from Howe to the staff of stenographers specified that delegates-at-large were to be designated "Hon." and all others simply as "Mr." except where listed with another title. There were lists of the arrival times of delegates in Chicago and trains to be met by staff members from the Roosevelt headquarters. Card indexes on the states reported every available scrap of information on each delegation, from the method of voting to the identity of Roosevelt agents within "enemy" delegations. If it was known that a man was susceptible to flattery, alcohol, pretty women, or photographs of himself with great statesmen, the fact was noted. It is doubtful that any preconvention campaign before or since—with the possible exception of John Kennedy's in 1960—was ever so painstakingly prepared.

In the week before the convention opened, Farley sent out a letter to all friendly delegates, signed in the green ink he always used: "We appreciate your fine work in assisting Franklin D. Roosevelt to secure the nomination . . ." Howe sent a similar letter to the same mailing list, with an autographed portrait of Roosevelt and a short recording of the Governor's "message, especially for you." The recorded voice purred,

> My dear friend, I wish it lay in my power to talk with you face to face on the eve of one of the most critical conventions that our party has ever held . . . I appreciate the high honor . . . I am a progressive in deed as well as word, in the truest and most Democratic sense . . . Please accept my assurances that you will always have the gratitude and friendship of Franklin Delano Roosevelt.

In contrast to the efficient stir in Albany, the "Stop Roosevelt" campaign seemed to be drifting aimlessly toward Chicago. There was still no polarization of agreement on a single candidate or on solutions to the nation's problems. Mayor Hague, Smith's designated floor leader at the convention, began a drumfire series of statements, attacking Roosevelt's alleged weakness, disloyalty, and inability to win. It added up to a haphazard, disorganized course of action, which was surprising, considering the proven organizational skills of men like Raskob, Shouse, and Smith. It was a suspicious alliance of uncomfortable bedfellows whose perspectives ranged from the old-fashioned populism of Alfalfa Bill Murray to the strait-laced fiscal conservatism of Harry Byrd, from the internationalism of Newton Baker to the isolationism of John Garner, and from the outcries for Repeal by Smith and Baker to the powdery Prohibitionist policy of Murray. No man was willing to defer to another, and no destination was in view beyond the destruction of the enemy.

On June 16, Roosevelt called his most trusted advisors to Hyde Park for a secret strategy countdown. Those meeting in the spacious, cluttered living room of the Roosevelt mansion were Howe, Flynn, Farley, Homer Cummings, former Chairman of the Democratic National Committee, Dan Roper, a Washington attorney, Robert Jackson of New Hampshire, and the Senators, Hull, Dill, Walsh, Wheeler, and Guffey. Cordell Hull read the platform, which he had helped to draft, for approval. After some discussion, it was decided to leave the question of fighting to suspend the two-thirds majority rule until the eve of the convention. The sense of the meeting, though, strongly favored a fight, for Howe's latest delegate-count showed Roosevelt with a clear majority of delegates, but still far short of two thirds.

The question of a permanent chairman for the convention was introduced by Burton Wheeler, who told Roosevelt that he would never be nominated if Jouett Shouse was named to that important post. Roosevelt agreed to back Walsh, who had chaired the exhausting 1924 convention and also presided over the Teapot Dome investigation. To pit Walsh against Shouse, whose name had been endorsed by the National Committee to be permanent chairman, was inviting trouble. There would certainly be a hot fight on the floor of the convention, and Roosevelt was sure to be vilified by Smith and the other sponsors of Shouse, but getting a friendly gavel, the conferees agreed, was absolutely essential.

Since Roosevelt had the delegate strength to control the machinery of the convention and dominate its committees, Cordell Hull was chosen to be chairman of the Platform Committee, and Bruce Kremer of Montana to head the Rules Committee. Two other committee nominations were left open for Farley to offer Paul McNutt in his last-minute bid for Indiana's delegates. Shaggy, aggressive Arthur Mullen of Nebraska was approved as Roosevelt's floor leader.

Certain key men in the Roosevelt organization were assigned to shadow leaders of the "Stop Roosevelt" coalition, to keep up a tattoo of propaganda and to watch for any signs of weakening as the delegates caucused and balloted. Wherever possible, these assignments were made on the basis of friendship or association. Roper was attached to his friend, McAdoo, for the duration of the convention, and Joe Kennedy was instructed to stay close to the observers and representatives of Hearst, his sometime business associate. Farley was dispatched to Sam Rayburn, Garner's campaign manager, and Howe opted for Harry Byrd. No ambassadors were assigned to the Smith-Raskob group, but Farley and Ed Flynn agreed to keep up a loose relationship with the leaders of the Tammany delegation.

The question of who should deliver the first nominating speech for Roosevelt had been caroming off the Hudson heights for weeks. Normally, but not invariably, the first nomination is made by a man of some stature in public life. Harry Byrd had already selected Senator Carter Glass, Albert Ritchie's choice was Senator Millard Tydings, and Governor Ely had agreed to say the honeyed words for Al Smith.

Roosevelt's first choice for the honor was Claude Bowers, the journalist and historian. Bowers begged off because he feared the wrath of his employer, Hearst. Senator Robert Wagner, the popular champion of labor, was Roosevelt's second choice. Wagner was afraid of the reaction of Tammany Hall, though, and after John Curry, the Tammany leader, called on Roosevelt to say that Wagner was a distasteful choice and would be embarrassing to the organization, his name was dropped. "Wagner had no nerve," Farley explains. "He and Roosevelt were never very close anyway." It began to look as though Roosevelt could not find any man to nominate him.

The next candidate Roosevelt picked was Tom Dowd, a legislator from Salamanca, New York. Farley objected and countered with the name of Judge John E. Mack of Poughkeepsie, an old friend and neighbor of Roosevelt. "I explained to him," Farley recalls, "that 'Mack'll take the speech that's prepared for him and deliver it. Tom is Irish. He'll talk all night.' " So John Mack got the nod.

It was, in some ways, a curious selection. Mack was Irish, too, though not a marathon speaker, and unknown outside of New York state. His only previous brushes with national fame had been two sensational trials of the 1920s, when he served as defense attorney for Mrs. Anne Urquhart Stillman against the divorce suit brought by her husband, James Stillman, and again as defense counsel for Edward W. ("Daddy") Browning in the separation suit brought by his wife, Frances ("Peaches") Browning. Stillman, a New York banker and a member of the Rockefeller family, had charged that his son, Guy, was actually the illegitimate child of his wife and Fred Beauvais, a Canadian trapper. After six years of litigation, Mack won his case and the child was declared Stillman's legitimate son and heir. Peaches Browning was fifteen years old when she married Daddy Browning, fifty-one, a wealthy real estate man, and left him after six bizarre, well-publicized months of marriage. Again Mack won his case for Browning. Both trials were sordid sensations of the decade, provender for the tabloid press for many months.

Judge Mack had one other brief moment in the limelight. In 1910 Dutchess County, traditionally a Republican fastness, was politically split by Theodore Roosevelt's schismatic Bull Moose Party, which was in open rebellion against William Howard Taft and the regular Republicans. Mack, the county's Democratic chairman, saw a chance for a Democratic victory and persuaded his neighbor, the twenty-eight-year-old Franklin Roosevelt, to run for the State Senate. Mack made the first nominating speech for him. Roosevelt won the party's nomination over the Tammany candidate, one Blue-Eyed Billy Sheehan, and, with Mack's backing and counsel, went on to victory over the divided Republicans. It was a surprise victory that attracted brief notice in the nation's press, and it started Roosevelt on his political career. While the choice of Judge Mack puzzled some of Roosevelt's advisors, who would have preferred a more famous name, it was easily understandable in Hyde Park. Three days later, as Farley and Flynn were packing to leave for Chicago, Roosevelt announced the selection of his "old friend and neighbor."

CHAPTER 6

THE REPUBLICAN CONVENTION

The Great Depression was the gravest issue confronting the nation and the world when 2,326 Republican delegates, with their families, aides and friends, assembled in Chicago in early June, but the general attitude of the convention was "What depression?" "An eavesdropper," wrote Raymond Daniell in *The New York Times*, "would seldom guess that the country was passing through a serious economic crisis. Unemployment and the depression are seldom mentioned, except by the serious-minded elder statesmen." In the platform which the convention's Resolutions Committee eventually hammered out in accordance with President Hoover's instructions, the issue was dismissed in two sentences: "The supremely important problem is to break [its] back. The patience and courage of the people have been severely tested."

And that was the extent of the convention's concern with the Depression. The party assumed no responsibility for the relief of the nearly twelve million unemployed citizens who were on the edge of starvation and social upheaval. It was a "problem of state and local responsibility," the platform stated. "The party is opposed to the Federal Government entering directly into the field of private charity."

But the Depression would not be ignored. Its phantom hand was everywhere in evidence in Chicago. Panhandling, unemployed men accosted delegates under the bunting-draped streetlights of Michigan Avenue. Ordinary delegates swarmed curiously through the lobbies of the big, elegant hotels, but they checked into the cheaper hotels and rooming houses on the seamy side of The Loop. The expensive restaurants and hotel dining rooms of the city were half-empty at meal times; the rank and file of the delegates sought out the meanest cafeterias and diners. The city fathers, who had put up $150,000 to lure the convention to Chicago, optimistically expected 125,000 visitors, each spending ten dollars a day. Both expectations were dashed. The Republican National Committee advertised "season tickets" to the galleries of the convention hall for hundred-dollar contributions to the party's campaign fund, but when the public's response was somewhat less than an avalanche, the price was hastily cut to forty dollars. Even then, the galleries were less than half filled when the convention was gavelled to order, and eventually Mayor Cermak opened the doors to anyone who wanted to come in off the streets.

Senator Simeon D. Fess of Ohio, an elderly statesman who wore a large gold badge, beribboned pince-nez and the formal attire of an earlier generation, was the Chairman of the Republican National Committee and nominally in charge of the convention. But the actual management came from the White House. Lawrence Richey, President Hoover's confidential secretary and field commander, arrived in Chicago early and immediately went into seclusion in a suite at the Congress Hotel, the convention headquarters. The resolutions of the platform, the selection of the candidates, the whole above-it-all tone of the convention were dictated by the man in the White House and enforced by his agent on the scene, Richey. This was not at all unusual; it is a hallowed political tradition that incumbent Presidents may dominate their party's conventions, select the candidates, and dictate the resolutions. And, unpopular though he undoubtedly was, even among many of his fellow Republicans, Herbert Hoover was still in firm control of the GOP's apparatus.

There were, to be sure, a few outbursts, some weak protests. Jane Addams, the aged suffragette, led a peace demonstration in the streets. An effigy of "Old Man Prohibition" was dumped into Lake Michigan by the Crusaders, a Wet organization, and beautiful women accosted delegates in the hotel lobbies, pinning Repeal buttons on their lapels. "If a man will just look doubtful, he can get a lot of attention," wrote the humorist, Will Rogers.

There were some signs of unrest from the floor of the convention, too. A movement to unseat Vice President Charles Curtis and nominate Charles

Gates Dawes (who had served as Coolidge's Vice President and Hoover's Ambassador to the Court of St. James's) was shortstopped by Dawes's refusal to let his name be placed in nomination, and by a telephone call from the White House. Curtis, a mild, genial bachelor, was the model of a "Throttlebottom" Vice President, and his chief sins were the fact that he was the first non-Anglo-Saxon Vice President in history, and the ludicrous public battle his ambitious sister and official hostess, Mrs. Edward Everett (Dolly) Gann, had waged with Mrs. Nicholas Longworth, wife of the former Speaker of the House and daughter of Theodore Roosevelt, over who should be declared the Second Lady of the Land. Dolly Gann was present at the convention, in a front-row box, accompanied by her publicity-shy husband, to cheer on the Curtis partisans. Alice Longworth was also present.

When it came to a vote, the fiat from the White House was obeyed, and Curtis was renominated, 634¼ votes to 401½. The nomination would not have passed on the first ballot, however, if Pennsylvania's delegation had not switched its seventy-five votes from General Edward Martin, the State Chairman, to Curtis. The vote was clearly the result of fear of the loss of political jobs and other favors that the President could bestow or withhold, and not of any great enthusiasm for Charles Curtis.

The convention was staged in the vast new Chicago Stadium, which was appropriately fitted out with four miles of red, white and blue bunting, shields of the forty-eight states, 2,100 flags, and a lone portrait of George Washington, surmounted by a large gold eagle. Since 1932 was the bicentennial anniversary of Washington's birth, and any number of special tributes and celebrations were being held across the nation, the portrait was entirely fitting, but what puzzled reporters when they arrived at the stadium was the fact that there was no portrait of Herbert Hoover, a most unconventional omission. Twelve concession stands ministered to the hungry and the thirsty, three thousand at a time. Andy Frain, the Chicago impresario, provided a legion of 150 ushers, with instructions to admit only the officially blessed, and to firmly bar such interlopers as Dr. Joseph Irwin France of Maryland, a political eccentric and former Senator, who was Hoover's only challenger for the Presidential nomination.

The press of the nation and the world was present in record-breaking numbers, with over six hundred reporters and correspondents, led by such luminaries as Arthur Krock, H. L. Mencken, William Allen White, Elmer Davis and Mark Sullivan. Foreign correspondents, led by the London *Times's* distinguished Washington bureau chief, Sir Wilmott Lewis, came to Chicago in unprecedented numbers and were, as foreign observers usually

are, completely bewildered by the strange and gaudy American spectacle.*
A post office branch was installed in the stadium, along with 425 extra telephones and telegraph facilities chattering out 400,000 words an hour to newspapers and magazines throughout the world.

Television was no more than a flickering experiment in 1932, but the presence and growing importance of radio was emphasized at the convention by clusters of sound discs hanging over the center of the stadium. The new-fangled medium had been introduced to political conventions in 1924, when some three million listeners along the Atlantic seaboard heard the nominations of Calvin Coolidge and John W. Davis.† In eight years, radio had advanced from a gadget to a communications medium that challenged the printed press. Static had been eliminated, except during thunderstorms, and 35,000 ground lines were run into Chicago to feed the news back to the networks. Scores of newscasters, whose names were already becoming familiar to the listening public, were on hand—Lowell Thomas, William Hard, H. V. Kaltenborn, David Lawrence, and the venerable Frederick William Wile. Floyd Gibbons, the dashing, one-eyed Hearst correspondent, spotted celebrities from the floor for NBC. Most of the radio reporters broadcast from Chicago Stadium four times a day—the gavel-to-gavel coverage of political conventions was yet to come. During lulls (and there were many) in the convention proceedings, CBS pages scurried through the aisles, offering the new lapel microphones to delegates who wanted to talk (and there

---

* *In 1952, when Alistair Cooke, the brilliant correspondent for* The Guardian *(then* The Manchester Guardian*) came to Chicago to report on the first political conventions he had attended, he disguised himself in a sport shirt and sun glasses so that he looked, or so he thought, like an authentic native, and went to the Stockyards Arena, where the Republicans were convening. From the press gallery, he took one look at the writhing, deafening bedlam below and fled to his hotel room, where he covered the rest of the convention via television.*

† *At the exhausting Democratic convention of 1924, H. L. Mencken once recalled, he and a friend, Richard V. Oulahan of* The New York Times, *decided to avail themselves of a guest card to the Union Club, across the street from Madison Square Garden, where they could find the cooling comforts of electric fans and a bartender—who loftily ignored the existence of Prohibition—and listen to the convention on radio. The two sat and sipped and listened while the clerk droned out the fortieth roll call. "Alabama," barked the clerk. "Alabama casts twenty-four votes for Underwood," came the reply. Then they heard a familiar voice, full of sorghum of the deep South, in what had become a roll-call litany: "Mistah Cheaman, Ah demand that the delegation be polled!" "At that moment," said Mencken, "we heard the voice of the convention chairman, Senator Tom Walsh, utter one word—'SHIT!' We sprang from our chairs, raced across the street and into the Garden, just in time to see Walsh's face turning a deep shade of purple, as he stared at the microphone in front of him and slowly realized that fifty thousand listeners from Richmond to Boston had heard him."*

were many). "Radio is going to revolutionize our political speaking," David Lloyd George, the wartime Prime Minister of Britain, had predicted at a Lotos Club dinner. "It is going to circumscribe the physical activities of our politicians, and will give them a little more time to think what they are to say."

The convention got under way to the crash of Simeon Fess's gavel, and proceeded montonously and exactly as scheduled by President Hoover. Even on small matters, such as the seating of contested delegations, the President had his way. When the Credentials Committee presented its report, it unseated the South Carolina delegation headed by Joseph ("Tieless Joe") Talbert, a veteran political boss and a national committeeman. The Credentials Committee had previously approved the Talbert delegation, but when the word was flashed from Washington that Tieless Joe had incurred the wrath of Hoover during an attempted 1929 purge of the Republican Party in the South, and was *non grata,* the committee hastily reversed itself and admitted the rival delegation.

When the name of Hoover was invoked for the first time, during the keynote address by Senator Lester Jesse Dickinson of Iowa, the delegates responded with faint and listless applause. That night Representative Bertrand Snell, the convention's permanent chairman, quietly informed the forty-eight delegation chiefs that he expected more enthusiasm when he mentioned the President's name. The following day, when Snell spoke of "the one man in America who has furnished leadership in this great crisis—Herbert Hoover," the delegates rose as if urged by a thousand cattle prods and bellowed their praise for the man in the White House. The band struck up "Iowa," the Hamilton, Ohio, Glee Club sang out, and a proper demonstration began.

Chairman Snell, a portly cheesemaker from Potsdam, New York, directed the convention proceedings authoritatively and efficiently, using a bung-starter, of all things, as a gavel. Speech after banal speech, resolution after bland resolution was ticked off, in one of the dullest political conventions ever. There was just one issue that touched off a flash of insurgency and brought the convention momentarily to life: the party's position on repealing the Eighteenth Amendment.

The Republicans, like the nation itself, were passionately divided on the issue. The Eastern, New England, and most Midwestern states were strongly in favor of legalizing liquor and banishing the Eighteenth Amendment from the Constitution. The fundamentalist South and the rural West were just as hotly convinced that drinking and trafficking spirits was a sin and should not be allowed—although many a Southern Baptist or Methodist piously voted the Dry ticket and still drank his fill in moonshine. The Republican Party had been the sponsor of the Eighteenth Amendment, moreover, and was for twelve years the defender of Prohibition. And that devout Quaker, Herbert Hoover, was the driest of the Drys.*

The delegations were a true reflection of the sentiment in the states they represented; New England, New York, New Jersey, Pennsylvania, Indiana, and Illinois were, as *Time* put it, "sopping wet" delegations; the South was Saharan Dry, and the other states were divided. Hoover was determined that the convention would not endorse Repeal in the party platform, and the Wet delegates were just as adamant that it would. The Resolutions Committee, under the chairmanship of James Rudolph Garfield, the son of the martyred President, appointed a subcommittee of seventeen to deal with the question of Repeal. Secretary of the Treasury Ogden Mills was the designated spokesman for the White House, and the other members of the subcommittee were all Cabinet members or allies of the President. In the ornate Florentine Room of the Congress Hotel, the subcommittee listened briefly to the leading spokesmen for Repeal—Nicholas Murray Butler, president of Columbia University, and Senator Hiram Bingham of Connecticut—and for Retention—Dr. A. C. Miller, a bearded Anti-Saloon League official, and Methodist Bishop James Cannon, Jr.—and then labored for twenty-four hours on a resolution that would satisfy both the man in the White House and the advocates of Demon Rum. "If the convention stops short of Repeal and the Democrats advocate it," warned Dr. Butler, "our nomination won't be worth the paper it is written on."

The declaration the subcommittee eventually produced and dutifully telephoned to Washington for official approval was an evasive compromise, recommending a referendum of the states which, if two thirds voted for Repeal, would abolish the Eighteenth Amendment only in those States that wanted to abolish it. The five-hundred-word resolution was studded with compromises and loopholes:

> We therefore believe that the people should have an opportunity to
> pass upon a proposed amendment, the provision of which, while retain-
> ing in the Federal Government power to preserve the gains already

* *In his mellow old age, ironically, Hoover had a mild heart ailment, and his doctor recommended two cocktails before dinner as a relaxant. The ex-President obediently sampled several mixed drinks, decided he liked dry martinis and, according to* The New Yorker, *increased the prescription to three drinks before dinner and one or two before lunch.*

made in dealing with the evils inherent in the liquor traffic, shall allow States to deal with the problem as their citizens may determine but subject always to the power of the Federal Government to protect those States where Prohibition may exist and safeguard our citizens everywhere from the return of the saloon . . .

It was a declaration designed to appeal to all men, and, although it won the grudging imprimatur of the President, it pleased no one at the convention. Senator Bingham wrote a minority report, demanding immediate repeal, and when the majority resolution, incorporated into the party platform, came to a vote, the listless convention suddenly came to life.

The galleries were nearly filled for the first time—with fifteen thousand strident advocates of Repeal. As soon as Chairman Garfield uttered the words, "Eighteenth Amendment," the air was filled with boos and hisses. Wet delegates on the floor demonstrated, with strings of beer steins and a chorus of "How Dry I Am." Garfield snapped at his hecklers: "The great backlog of oak that gives heat to the home is not disturbed by the prattling of the kindling." After two hours of steaming debate and seventeen speeches, the convention rejected the Bingham minority report and accepted the committee's watery resolution by a vote of 681 to 472. It was not a popular vote, but a mustering out of the arid South and the pressuring into line of many delegates who held appointive offices.

As a measure of the times, the hotels of Chicago had stockpiled huge supplies of bootlegged liquor and were dispensing it to delegates through room service at the rate of twelve dollars for a quart of Scotch, ten dollars for Bourbon, and two dollars for gin.

After the uproar over the Repeal plank, the convention apathetically approved the entire platform, a cumbersome, nine thousand-word document that promised something for just about every group in the United States. Bank deposits would be protected. The farmer would be paid more for his products, perhaps. Tariffs would remain high. A study would be made to find solutions to the problems of war veterans. America would join the World Court. Wages would be high. The working day and working week would be shorter. The government would be reorganized. Labor's right to collective bargaining was approved. And the Democrats were inept: "The vagaries of the Democratic House offer characteristic and appalling proof of the existing incapacity of that party for leadership in a national crisis. Individualism running amok, has displaced party discipline. . . ." Summing it up, Walter Lippmann wrote,

Much as they would like to create the impression, it would not be true to say that the Hoover conservatism presents a body of coherent conservative principles. Far from it. Anyone who will expose himself to the pain of reading the platform from beginning to end will discover that Mr. Hoover has long since abandoned his old faith in rugged individualism. His platform is a document of indefatigable paternalism. Its spirit is that of the Great White Father providing help for all his people. Every conceivable interest which has votes is offered protection, or subsidies, or access of some kind to the Treasury.

Herbert Hoover's own renomination was a masterpiece of political stagecraft. When his name was placed in nomination, kleig lights were switched on, and Delegate Louis B. Mayer, the film producer, projected slides of the President on screens at each end of the auditorium. The carefully organized demonstration went off as programmed, with a director on the rostrum, flashing numbered placards to indicate the descent of balloons, band numbers, organ numbers, light displays, and the procession of marchers.

At the end of the demonstration, Delegate Lawritz B. Sandblast approached the microphone to place the name of Dr. France in nomination. As he opened his mouth, the amplifying system went dead, and his speech went unheard. When France himself tried to reach the platform, Andy Frain's muscular ushers and the police hustled him out of the stadium. The amplifiers were thereupon switched on again, and the seven seconding speeches, praising the President to the sky, went on as scheduled. One seconder, a Chicago Negro, Roscoe E. Simmons, even brought the endorsement of Abraham Lincoln, which he said he had gotten while standing before the tomb of the Emancipator: "He seemed to say . . . 'Go and speak to those who still gather in my name. Say that I dwell about the stout and burdened heart that bears the nation on it. And if you see him, speak to Hoover for me and say that his road is the one I traveled.'" Earlier, Chairman Snell had likened Hoover to George Washington, on the grounds that both men were engineers.

The roll call was orderly and routine. There were just 23½ votes against Hoover, divided among five favorite sons and mavericks. The President was overwhelmingly nominated for a second term by 1,126½ votes. As the convention wound up its business, Will Rogers reported, "The whole town is on edge, waiting for the Democrats to come. You know at a big dinner, when you sit down there is nothing on the table but little individual dishes of nuts. Well, that's what this Republican convention is, before a big dinner; it's the nertz." Added Arthur Krock: "To all this the national assembly of the Democrats will provide the contrast of scarlet to dull gray . . ."

On Broadway, bookmaker Jack Doyle quoted betting odds of three to five against Herbert Hoover's reelection.

CHAPTER 7

THE EVE
OF BATTLE

In the week-long entr'acte between the end of the Republican convention and the Democrats' noisy arrival onstage, the nation twittered like a dovecote with political talk and political plans. Other news in the papers was banished from the front pages. Amelia Earhart Putnam was given a traditional ticker-tape welcome in New York after her triumphant solo flight to Paris. Helen Wills Moody won her fifth tennis singles championship at Wimbledon. Babe Ruth slammed out his nineteenth home run of the baseball season, to crush the Cleveland Indians, and Jack Sharkey, a Boston bartender, outpointed Max Schmeling, the German challenger, to win the world's heavyweight boxing championship before a wildly partisan audience of seventy thousand. In Thailand (then called Siam) King Prajadhipok meekly accepted the restrictions imposed by an army coup d'état and ended one of the world's last absolute monarchies.

Grand Hotel was the big attraction in the movie palaces. For those who could afford a vacation, the Ward Line advertised a six-and-a-half day all-expense cruise to Havana for $65. Wallach's, the Fifth Avenue men's store, was selling straw hats for $1.85, seersucker suits for $10, and Florsheim shoes for $6.85. Bernarr McFadden's New York *Graphic,* sleaziest of the tabloids and birthplace of Walter Winchell's gossip column, published its last edition and filed a petition of bankruptcy. Potatoes were priced at five pounds for ten cents, ham, fifteen cents a pound, Uneeda biscuits, two packages for seven cents, imported sardines, five cents a can, and butter and coffee were both nineteen cents a pound at the A & P. Cigarettes cost twenty-five cents for two packs.

In Milwaukee, the Socialist Party held its convention and, to the surprise of no one, nominated Norman Thomas, the uncommon champion of the common man, as its Presidential candidate. Thomas was the perennial Socialist candidate and, for a generation, the refuge of voters of both conservative and radical persuasion who could not stomach either the Republican or the Democratic candidates. In November 1932, Thomas would win 350,000 votes—the largest plurality in his six campaigns and the largest number of votes ever cast for a Socialist in the United States.

The biggest news was emanating from Chicago, Washington, Albany, and the other centers where the Democrats were readying their battle plans. In the Empire State Building, Al Smith held a final strategy meeting with Governor Ely and Jouett Shouse. When reporters asked Ely if he would refer to Smith as The Happy Warrior in his nominating speech, he snapped, "We've graduated from that high school stuff, I hope."

In Washington, Speaker Garner served Bourbon highballs to his Texas and California strategists in The Board of Education and arranged a system of communications with Representative Sam Rayburn, the canny Texan he had selected to manage his campaign in Chicago. Garner had decided that going to the convention himself would be poor strategy. Congress was still in session, and Garner did not want to expose himself to any of the dissidents or to envoys from Roosevelt. So he would sit the convention out in Washington and stay incommunicado to everyone but Mister Sam. He told Rayburn that the one thing he wanted to avoid was a prolonged, deadlocked convention. If such a situation developed, Garner said, Rayburn was to use the ninety Texas and California ballots in any way he could to break the deadlock.

In Albany, the activity was intense. Busy lieutenants and couriers buzzed in and out of the Governor's Mansion like bees in cloverbloom. Louis Howe kept the long-distance telephones humming, as he checked with the leaders of the pledged delegations and argued with those of undecided or doubtful groups. Jim Farley took to the road again, in a last effort to corral the maverick delegations of Ohio, Indiana and Illinois. After the loss of California, Farley felt that Roosevelt's best, possibly his last, chance for a first-ballot victory would be to win over the votes of the three states. Although Illinois and Ohio were pledged to favorite sons, their ballots could easily be switched, after a token vote for the sons. Farley came bearing gifts, which he hoped to exchange for votes: the chairmanship of the prestigious Committee on Permanent Organization for Colonel Paul V. McNutt, and the promise of a job in Washington for Chicago's Mayor Cermak.

The advance men for the Al Smith coalition, he found, had been there before him. State functionaries who had been friendly to him on his previous trips were now reserved and noncommittal. It was apparent, he said, "that we were getting the foot." In Fort Wayne, Farley met with Earl Peters, one of Indiana's delegation leaders, and offered the chairmanship for McNutt in exchange for an instructed delegation, pledged to Roosevelt. Peters was dubious, but agreed to consult with McNutt. In Chicago, Farley had no better luck. Mayor Cermak told him that he could make no promises until Senator Ham Lewis had made up his mind about keeping his stance as a favorite son.

While he was in Chicago, Farley reserved the Presidential Suite at the Congress Hotel—then being occupied by Senator Fess—for the week of the Democratic Convention, and touched off a flurry of speculation in the press that Roosevelt might be planning to come to Chicago himself. But Farley was inscrutable about any plans the Governor might have in the near future.

When he returned to New York, Farley found a letter from McNutt that seemed to confirm his suspicions that Al Smith & Co. had been campaigning in the Middle West. "While Governor Roosevelt has many staunch supporters in this state," the letter said, "I find that an overwhelming majority of the Democratic leaders feel they should not be hampered by instructions . . ." Farley's last hope of tying up the nomination before the convention had vanished.

Roosevelt devoted as much time as he could to his busy aides and their plans and intelligence, but he was engrossed in a problem that was bound to affect his chances in Chicago, no matter how he solved it—the case of Jimmie Walker, the dapper playboy mayor of New York. Walker was the creature of Tammany Hall and the wise-cracking, high-living darling of the city's poor minorities. To most of the nation, however, he was the apotheosis of arrogant, corrupt, big city bossism. Throughout his political career, Roosevelt had always kept a gingerly distance from Tammany, carefully dissociating himself from the machine, yet doing nothing to offend its bosses if he could help it. It was an awkward, uncertain sort of political coexistence, and it helped sustain the charges of his enemies that Roosevelt was weak, shallow, and lacked courage. Whenever he had to deal with the sachems of Tammany, Roosevelt usually sent Howe or Farley as his emissary. In the context of the times, this was actually just pragmatic politics; no

honest Democratic politician in New York could have challenged Tammany
—or so it was believed—and survived. In Roosevelt's case, this wary *modus
vivendi* worked—as it had worked for Al Smith when he was governor—
until the scandals erupted.

The murder of a red-headed adventuress and the revelation that
New York City's Sheriff Thomas M. Farley (no relation to James Farley)
had banked $396,000 over a seven-year period in which he had earned just
$87,000 in salary, touched off the blaze. Governor Roosevelt fired Sheriff
Farley, but the flickering rumors about Mayor Walker himself would not
be quenched and led the Republicans in Albany to form a special legislative
committee to investigate. Judge Samuel Seabury, a meticulous, aristocratic
lawyer and a registered Democrat who had no love for Roosevelt and less
for Tammany Hall, was appointed chief investigator. His revelations shocked
the nation, destroyed Walker's credibility (although the faith of his New
York City following was utterly unshaken) and made Seabury famous. On
the witness stand, Walker was shifty and evasive, trying to wisecrack his way
out of damning disclosures and seemingly unanswerable questions.

Judge Seabury bore in mercilessly, revealing that municipal contracts
had been let to "friendly" firms, headed by cronies of the Mayor, and that
Walker had received vast "loans" in return, to finance his high living in New
York and expensive trips to Europe. The Mayor's sixty-dollar-a-week book-
keeper, who vanished on the eve of the investigation, had deposited $961,000
in a special bank account, which he used to pay many of Jimmie Walker's
bills.

The Seabury Investigation was well covered by the nation's newspapers and wire services,* and the public indignation was enormous. The
investigation ended in May 1932, and the full bill of charges was presented
to Governor Roosevelt by Judge Seabury.

Roosevelt's reaction was described by Alfred B. Rollins, Jr., in his
book, *Roosevelt and Howe*, as "almost paranoic." The whole affair, Roosevelt protested, was just a plot to upset his political plans. "This fellow
Seabury," he complained, "is merely trying to perpetrate another political
play to embarrass me." That may well have been one of Seabury's motives,
one reason for his precise, preconvention timing. A friendlier investigator
would have waited a few weeks. Whatever his reasons, Seabury journeyed
to Albany and presented a fifteen-count indictment to Roosevelt, with no

* One young reporter, John Boettiger of the Chicago Daily News, met Roosevelt's daughter, Anna Roosevelt Dall, at the hearings, and married her soon after. They were subse-
quently divorced. Years later, the mentally deranged Boettiger escaped from his male nurse
and leaped to his death from a New York hotel room.

recommendations. Roosevelt was skewered on a three-horned dilemma. If he called for Walker's head, Tammany's bloc of delegates would go to the eager Smith. If he dismissed the case against the Mayor, he would win Tammany's ballots, but lose the respect of the nation and the votes of uncounted delegates in Chicago. And finally, if he just ignored the matter and let it slide until after the convention, he would have to face the growing wrath of the press and public and the old charge that he was weak and unworthy of the Presidency.

"Samuel Seabury has maneuvered the governor into a position where he will be compelled to take action," said an anonymous New York delegate. "If he removes the mayor, he will lose a couple of hundred Tammany votes in New York City. If he leaves him in office, he is apt to lose the votes of an equal number who are eager to see the mayor thrown out of office. No matter what action he takes, he will lose enough votes to place his own state in the Hoover column."

On June 11, in reply to a letter from Dr. J. W. Harrison of San Antonio inquiring about the Walker case, Roosevelt wrote, "I have acted to the limits of my constitutional powers on all evidence of wrong-doing, and I shall continue to act, without regard to its influence on my political future." But he continued to hesitate and called in a battery of lawyers to analyze Seabury's charges and advise him what to do.

Roosevelt gloomed over the Seabury Report for two full weeks. Finally, on June 22, just five days before the Democrats met in Chicago, he sent the transcript of the report to Walker and demanded an explanation: "My dear Mayor: I am sending you herewith certain charges and analysis filed with me containing allegations relating to your conduct as Mayor of the City of New York. . . ."

The matter was by no means settled, but it was at least on ice until after the convention. Roosevelt had broken with Tammany and he had probably lost Tammany's convention votes, but he had redeemed himself at least partly in the eyes of the press and public. Later, in July, with the Democratic Convention behind him, Roosevelt called his own investigation in Albany, and Walker performed as badly as he had before the Seabury Investigation. After some desperate legal maneuvering and an appeal to the State Supreme Court, Jimmie Walker resigned as mayor, and went off hurriedly to European exile and political oblivion with his mistress, Broadway showgirl Betty Compton.

New York's Governor Franklin D. Roosevelt relaxes over solitaire
some months before the 1932 Democratic National Convention.

Above: Senator Alben Barkley of Kentucky gave the keynote address at the Democratic Convention. Barkley, who turned down the suggestion that he seek the Presidential nomination as a favorite son, is shown here with John J. Raskob, chairman of the Democratic National Committee. Below: Drafting the Democratic platform were some of the leading Democrats of the era: (*left to right*) Senator Carter Glass of Virginia, Senator David I. Walsh of Massachusetts, A. Mitchell Palmer, Wilson's Attorney General, Senator Burton K. Wheeler of Montana, Joseph C. O'Mahoney of Wyoming, Senator Cordell Hull of Tennessee, William Gibbs McAdoo of California, and William A. Comstock of Michigan.

United Press International Photo

Above: Newton D. Baker (*right*), seen conferring with James A. Farley, was among those contesting FDR for the 1932 Democratic Presidential nomination. Baker had been Secretary of War in Wilson's cabinet. Below: Alfred E. Smith, a major Roosevelt rival for the 1932 Democratic Presidential nomination, chats with a friend at Smith campaign headquarters at the Chicago Convention.

Courtesy Franklin D. Roosevelt Library (Acme)

Senator Tom Connally of Texas in action during the Democratic Convention.

Industrialist Owen D. Young, earlier mentioned as a possible Democratic Presidential nominee, supported FDR at the Chicago Convention.

Above: Mayor Jimmy Walker of New York City posed with fellow mayors Frank Hague (*left*) of Jersey City and Anton J. Cermak of Chicago. Walker cast his half vote for Al Smith. Below: The controversial Father Charles E. Coughlin, a Michigan supporter of FDR, addresses the Chicago nominating convention.

Oklahoma's Governor Alfalfa Bill Murray scrutinizes a new device, a lapel microphone worn by Convention pages. Murray received fifty-two votes on the first ballot for the Presidential nomination.

William Gibbs McAdoo, former Democratic senator from California, electrified the convention when he announced the switch of his state's forty-four votes from Garner to Roosevelt.

Speaker of the House John Nance Garner of Texas
was nominated as FDR's running mate.

FDR and family are greeted by James A. Farley at the Chicago airport after their flight from Albany. With FDR are his daughter, Anna Dall, FDR, Jr., James, and Elliott.

Louis Howe, FDR, and James A. Farley at the Democratic Convention, July 4, 1932.

FDR, son James, and James A. Farley share a light moment at the 1932 Democratic Convention. Just behind the microphone at the right is Will Rogers, who, though not a candidate, received twenty-two votes on the second ballot for the Presidential nomination.

On the next three pages: The contest for the Democratic Presidental nomination as seen through the eyes of contemporary cartoonists.

SOMETHING DOING

ANOTHER OF THOSE CHICAGO PINEAPPLES

The Unhappy Warrior's Retreat -:- -:- By War

Riding to Victory!

"HOOEY" LONG BROUGHT TO THE CONVENTION A SAMPLE OF HIS LOUISIANA GOVERNMENT AND THE ROOSEVELT FORCES ENDORSED IT!

SENATOR WALSH WHOSE VICTORY OVER SHOUSE FOR THE PERMANENT CHAIRMANSHIP DEMONSTRATED THE COMPLETE SUPREMACY OF THE ROOSEVELT FORCES

DURING THE RECESS.

The taste of victory.

CHAPTER 8

"WE HAVE ROOSEVELT LICKED NOW"

On June 20, Jim Farley, Ed Flynn, and a dozen members of Roosevelt's campaign staff arrived in Chicago and set up headquarters at the Congress Hotel. Farley had reserved sixty-two hotel rooms for the housing of staff workers, the entertainment and seduction of delegates and, wishfully, the launching of a bandwagon. The headquarters of Roosevelt and the other candidates occupied most of the Congress' second floor, which Chicagoans named "President's Row." Governor Ritchie was installed in the Florentine Room, and others were nearby—Byrd, Smith, Murray, Garner, Hamilton Lewis, Melvin Traylor, and Governor White of Ohio. Each headquarters swarmed with press officers, political aides, pretty girls dispensing coffee, campaign buttons, and literature, and oftentimes the candidate himself was present, hand outstretched and proselytizing pitch at the ready. Each headquarters exuded confidence. To the politically untutored, it was a bewildering experience just to wander from headquarters to headquarters and see a dozen or more sure-fire winners, each with his own rationalization of how he was going to storm the convention and win the Presidential nomination. Emerging from Farley's office, John W. Davis smilingly explained, "I'm just going around from cage to cage to look at the animals and pick out one to support. But I am not saying anything yet."

The Roosevelt headquarters was, unsurprisingly, the scene of the most feverish activity and the object of the most curiosity. On his arrival, Farley held a press conference for forty newspapermen and solemnly predicted a first-ballot nomination for Roosevelt, with 791 votes—twelve over the necessary two-thirds majority—including the thirty-six-vote Missouri delegation which, Farley claimed, would cast a courtesy vote for James Reed and then switch to Roosevelt before the end of the balloting. Other delegate nose-counts were not so optimistic, putting the man from Hyde Park anywhere from 80 to 150 votes short of the magic number. A week before the opening gavel, it was clear that, while Roosevelt undoubtedly had a substantial lead, many of Farley's claims were wishful. A dozen or more state delegations were anything but solidly behind his candidate. In some delegations, such as Mississippi, the balance for Roosevelt rested on a hairbreadth one-half vote, held by one wavering delegate. In others, such as New York, there was no way of telling which way the vital vote would go.

Tammany Hall was reported to hold the balance of power in the New York delegation, and, if Roosevelt should lose out in the first ballot, Farley reported, "the Tammany braves would be able to master their grief . . . Already, they were hinting that I had signed my own political death warrant by backing Roosevelt."

Newspapermen, and politicians in the "Stop Roosevelt" pool, were attracted to a large map of the United States prominently displayed on a wall of Roosevelt headquarters. The map was the idea of Frank Walker, who suggested it to Roosevelt as a means of persuading hesitant delegates to climb on the bandwagon. It showed those states "committed to Roosevelt" in red, and while many of the "commitments" were dubious and tentative, the map was sanguine enough to awe and perhaps win over any doubtful delegates who saw it. There was some comment on the fact that Farley's cartographer had colored Texas and California yellow. New York was an enigmatic white.

On June 21, in Washington, William A. Borah, the leonine senator from Idaho, and a towering figure in the populist prairie and mountain states, announced that he would not support Hoover for reelection because of the Republicans' flaccid stand on Prohibition. The announcement brought joy to the hearts of Democratic schemers in Chicago, who translated it into thousands upon thousands of switch-votes from the devoted followers of the messianic "Big Bill."

The whispering campaigns against Roosevelt and his rivals were intensifying. John O'Donnell, Philadelphia's minority council commissioner and chairman of the Democratic City Committee, reported that Frank Hague had come to Philadelphia and offered him "anything you want" to desert Roosevelt and support Smith. "I told him that I thought Roosevelt had a better chance of winning this year [than Smith had in 1928]," O'Donnell said. Boss Hague released a blistering denial.

James M. Callahan, member of the Democratic National Committee from Wisconsin and a backer of Al Smith, sent all the delegates to the convention photostatic copies of letters from Roosevelt and Farley to the organizers of the Roosevelt Southern Clubs, which purportedly showed that the Roosevelt movement in the South had received aid and support from the Ku Klux Klan. Roosevelt, in Albany, refused comment, saying that the charge was too absurd to warrant a reply.

In Washington, Senator George Moses of New Hampshire, a Republican leader in the Senate, and author of *Wild Jackasses I Have Known,* made a flat prediction: "Roosevelt, of course, will not be nominated. There will be a deadlock, chieftains will meet in the usual smoke-filled room, and Senator Bulkley of Ohio will be nominated." It was a surprising statement from a shrewd professional politician, for Robert J. Bulkley was a Harvard classmate and friend of Roosevelt's, and one of his most enthusiastic supporters. Along with Moses' statement, Chicago's newspapers carried another pronouncement, attributed to Jouett Shouse: "We have Roosevelt licked now."

By midweek the traffic to Chicago was reaching stampede proportions. Harry Byrd was the first avowed candidate to arrive, at the head of his machine-tooled delegation of Virginians. At the Baltimore & Ohio's Chicago terminal, he made a statement to the press which was true to the course of purse-string economy that would characterize him for the next thirty-five years in the United States Senate. "The menacing increase of the cost of government ranks among the foremost of our problems," Byrd said. "We cannot continue to pay fifty million dollars each day to our local, state and federal governments—one dollar out of every four we earn—without eventual bankruptcy."

From New York, six hundred Tammany Hall braves, families and friends steamed into Chicago on three special trains. Four hundred others followed on regularly scheduled trains, and 150 more made the hazardous—in 1932—trip by automobile. Al Smith arrived on a special car attached to the New York Central's elite Twentieth Century Limited five days before the convention opening, and was met by a mob that blocked his way through the La Salle Street Station for fifteen minutes. He was scarlet-faced, smiling and stubble-chinned (he had been afraid to use his old straight razor on the lurching train), and he doffed his straw hat and amiably signed autographs as police tried to clear a path for him. As he made his way through the crowd, Smith fielded the questions of reporters:

Q. Will you support the nominee of the convention, regardless . . . ?
A. I do not think it necessary to talk about that at this time.
Q. Who do you think the convention will nominate for President?
A. The convention will decide.
Q. Who is your preference for the nomination?
A. The Honorable Alfred E. Smith of New York.
Q. To insure Democratic success, what's the best thing the party can do?
A. Write an honest, clear, straightforward platform, and nominate me.

In reply to a question about his "Stop Roosevelt" movement, Smith answered evenly, "I do not know anything about a 'Stop Roosevelt' movement. I came here to combat a 'Stop Smith' movement which commenced a year and a half ago." A frown suddenly clouded his face, and the Happy Warrior complained, "Aw, let me go. I want to get a shave." He pulled his wife, whose face was almost covered by a large spray of orchids, through the milling crowd.

Tammany's leaders, John F. Curry and John McGooey, slipped quietly into Chicago in the vanguard of the Tammany delegation. They were the realization of a cartoonist's dream of big city bosses—both pudgy, florid, bald-headed men with ample white moustaches. Within minutes of his arrival in Chicago, Curry was closeted with Farley, and the rumor spread that Tammany Hall would not help Roosevelt, but would readily climb aboard a bandwagon if it looked as if there was no stopping him. Farley cheerfully added fuel to the rumors with a claim that all but four of the New York delegates would vote for his candidate. "That's just some of Jim Farley's ballyhoo," snorted Al Smith. He dismissed Farley's announcement of other states falling in line behind Roosevelt as a "bedtime story."

The delegations and the candidates continued to pour into Chicago. With hotel rooms at a premium, hundreds of delegates chose to sleep aboard their special trains in the railroad yards. Huey Long roared into town and announced that his docile, hand-picked delegation (which was challenged by another Louisiana group) was for Roosevelt, resubmission of the Prohibition Amendment to the states, and abrogation of the two-thirds majority rule. John Raskob, trying to preserve his official above-the-battle image, made a statement that mentioned no candidate and urged all good men to come to the aid of the party: "No such opportunity for victory as we enjoy today has presented itself to the Democratic Party since the Civil War."

Burton K. Wheeler, the Montana zealot who had been the first to urge Roosevelt to run, and William G. McAdoo, with their delegates, arrived on the same train. The arrival of Wheeler, a man with high political ambitions* of his own, coincided with a report that Roosevelt had offered him the Vice-Presidential nomination. The report alarmed Roosevelt, who wanted to buy votes with the Vice-Presidential nomination, and prompted him to send off a telegram to Farley:

> I UNDERSTAND THE CHICAGO EXAMINER SAYS I HAVE ASKED SENATOR BURTON K. WHEELER TO BECOME VICE PRESIDENTIAL CANDIDATE WITH ME THIS FALL. THIS STORY IS NOT TRUE. I HAVE ALREADY MADE IT CLEAR TO THE PRESS AND THE COUNTRY THAT I HAVE ASKED NO ONE TO BE MY RUNNING MATE AND THAT NO ONE HAS BEEN AUTHORIZED TO DO SO ON MY BEHALF.

This was patently untrue: both Farley and Howe had Roosevelt's power of attorney to offer the Vice Presidency to any one of several candidates, in return for the votes they controlled. This was, of course, and is considered a perfectly fair and honorable practice in the big leagues of politics.

From New York, Joseph Patrick Kennedy, the red-headed, politically bred millionaire who had known Roosevelt during the war in the Navy Department, flew to Albany for lunch and final instructions from the Governor, before boarding the Twentieth Century for Chicago.

As the week drew to a close, Chicago was as charged with excitement and speculation as a Broadway theater when the lights dim on the opening night of a major play. The Smith headquarters was as crowded with visitors and speculation as the Roosevelt suite. "Twenty percent cooler in Smith Headquarters," announced a poster in the lobby of the Congress. Al Smith held a press conference to discuss Farley's map. Besides being inaccurate, he said, the states shown in red had very small populations and little ballot strength at the convention. "It reminds me of Champ Clark's map, in 1912," added McAdoo.

Mayor Hague fired the opening gun of his convention attack on the Roosevelt candidacy in a mimeographed statement which he distributed to the press:

---

* *He bolted the Democratic Party briefly in 1924 to run for the Vice Presidency in the Progressive Party's brief fling at national politics, with the senior Robert LaFollette heading the ticket.*

Governor Roosevelt, if nominated, has no chance of winning in November. He cannot carry a single state east of the Mississippi . . . The Democratic Party has a golden opportunity, but for the party to select the weakest man cannot bring success. Governor Roosevelt has utterly failed in his last two attempts [the Massachusetts and California primaries] to sell himself to the people . . . Why consider the one man who is weakest in the eyes of the rank and file?

Response from the Roosevelt camp was immediate and bitter. "It is the wail of the lost," said A. Mitchell Palmer. "Just the funeral march—the last screech of defeat!" screeched Huey Long. "All Frank Hague knows is the road to Manhattan!"

Roosevelt's own public reaction was calm and above the battle. When Farley telephoned him and read Hague's words, Roosevelt dictated a reply, but put the words in Farley's mouth: "Governor Roosevelt's friends have not come to Chicago to criticize, cry down or defame any Democrat from any part of the country. This, I believe, is sufficient answer to Mr. Hague's statement."

The Smith forces continued to fire away at Roosevelt, but it was more the rooftop fire of snipers than the salvos and volleys of a well-organized alliance. The anti-Roosevelt coalition existed, to be sure, but it lacked an over-all plan and command and seemed, to seasoned journalists and impartial politicians, to be a very loose association of *presidenciables,* each pursuing his own ambitions, each suspicious of the other, none willing to follow another. Smith's announcement of his own serious candidacy, on his arrival in Chicago, was a stunning blow to some of his allies—especially Albert Ritchie—who had naïvely believed his protests that he was merely a surrogate candidate, the custodian of a sizable number of delegate votes, who would throw his support to the nebulous candidate who would emerge from the coalition.

Every day the dissident candidates and favorite sons, or their spokesmen, met secretly at a penthouse three miles from the convention headquarters. The meetings were not so much the coordinating sessions of a grand alliance, working out a joint strategy, as wary exchanges of information and rumor. Nor were they very secret; Farley was fully informed about them.

Smith headquarters announced that a private poll of delegates had revealed that Roosevelt could command no more than 570 votes—eight less than a simple majority and 207 short of a two-thirds majority. A Smith-produced sign in hotel lobbies ridiculed Farley's strength map, and twice coupled the word "red" with Roosevelt's name—a not-so-subtle innuendo that the candidate was somehow linked with communism.

Al Smith himself commuted between the golf course and the conference room of his headquarters. He met with Mayor Cermak and told him that, as a candidate, Roosevelt was doomed to defeat. He lunched with Curry, McGooey, Raskob, Shouse, and Hague. He was visited by Bernard Baruch and his brother, Sailing Baruch, and by Herbert Bayard Swope, former managing editor of the defunct New York *World* and then serving as a highly-paid public relations consultant for Baruch.

The corridors of the second floor of the Congress were clogged with people struggling to gain entrance to the various headquarters. Throngs of the curious queued up at the entrance of Murray's headquarters to get a glimpse of the grizzled, unkempt Alfalfa Bill, clad in a rumpled Palm Beach suit and—incongruously, in the balmy June weather—a woolen muffler, chewing on a cigar butt, drinking quarts of jet-black coffee and discussing farm subsidies, economic problems or whatever topic turned up with whoever turned up. When he felt fatigued, Murray simply stretched out on a cot and held forth from there. Oklahoma, he said, would vote for Roosevelt only "after frost—and frost down our way don't come until after election."

In the corridor, the California delegation paraded in honor of the absent Garner, accompanied by the Chicago Board of Trade band and "California, Here I Come." In Washington, Garner belatedly announced that he was striking a blow for liberty and advocating Repeal. It was an announcement that was not likely to appeal to his Southern admirers, but Garner needed northern votes, and Sam Rayburn felt that he had to make his position clear if he was to make any progress in the big, populous Northern states.

In a quiet, unpublicized suite, a floor above the madding second floor of the Congress, one of Newton Baker's aides, Colonel Lemuel P. Ayres of Cleveland, established a clandestine headquarters and began rounding up votes. Hundreds of telegrams, written by Baruch and Swope, advocating Baker's candidacy, poured into every delegation. They had considerable success: by the time the convention was ready to cast its first ballots, Baker had cornered nine and a half of Mississippi's twenty votes—just one ballot short of taking over that unit-ruled delegation—and countless pledges of second-choice, or after-Roosevelt votes. Baker kept his distance, in Cleveland, and when a reporter asked him who he thought would win the nomination, he replied loftily, "I never speculate on that question."

The last celebrities and delegates reached Chicago on the eve of the convention. Two days after he had received Franklin Roosevelt's letter asking him to answer the charges of scandal, Delegate Jimmie Walker, with his pet Japanese spaniel and a party of three, boarded a private railroad car attached to the Commodore Vanderbilt. Swarms of his faithful constituents jammed Grand Central Terminal to give him an enthusiastic send-off. The Mayor was dressed in a stylish gray suit and a jaunty fedora, and seemed to be as self-possessed and cocky as ever. When a photographer said, "Move over, please, we can't see very well," Jimmie grinned and cracked, "I can't Seabury well myself."

The next morning Chicago turned out with a warm reception and a band playing the inevitable "Sidewalks of New York." But Walker passed up the Drake Hotel, headquarters of the New York delegation and over-flowing with his Tammany brethren, to be the guest at the lakeside home of Vincent Bendix, the manufacturer, and spent most of the convention week attending the races, dancing, and avoiding the limelight. His failure to check in at the Drake may have been an act of prudence, though, for another New Yorker, who described himself as an "independent Democrat" had already been occupying a suite there for several days: Judge Samuel Seabury.

Governor Ritchie, arriving in Chicago with the Maryland delegation on a special eleven-car train, was mobbed by supporters at the station and lost a shoe in the crush. For puzzling reasons, the city gave him its warmest welcome; 100,000 people turned out to applaud Ritchie and shower him with confetti and ticker-tape on his ride to his hotel.

Two days before the convention opened, Bernard Baruch arranged a meeting between Smith and McAdoo at his Blackstone Hotel suite. When Baruch called him with the invitation, Smith replied, "Bernie, I don't like him and I won't be comfortable while I'm with him, but in this fight I would sleep with a Chinaman to win, and I'll come."

The two men had not seen one another since their great struggle for the nomination eight years before, and their bitterness and mutual distrust had not subsided. According to the Baltimore *Sun* columnist, Frank R. Kent, the meeting was as awkward and uneasy as Al Smith had predicted it would be. When·Smith entered Baruch's apartment, McAdoo leaped up and greeted him with outstretched hand. "How are you, how are you?" he asked.

"Out of sight, out of sight," Smith replied, accepting McAdoo's hand.

"Well," said McAdoo, "we both got licked."

"Yes, we both got licked," said Smith wryly, "but it was better for me to beat you and you to beat me than for either of us to take a fall from Coolidge."

After a few minutes of nervous pleasantries, the two implacable enemies and Baruch went to the luncheon table and a discussion of the real purpose of their meeting. "Well," asked McAdoo, "what are you going to do out here?"

"I'm going to level with you," said Smith. "We're both against Roosevelt, or you wouldn't be here. Is that right?" McAdoo agreed that it was. "All right," said Smith, "if we get together we can beat this feller . . . If we go to the fifth ballot, we've got him licked. All right. Then my candidacy is out the window. I can't be nominated, but we can then sit around a table and get together on a candidate."

McAdoo was wary. "When you sit around the table," he asked, "will I be there?"

"If you're not there I won't be either," said Smith. On that note the meeting ended. The two men shook hands again, posed for photographers, and Smith went back to the Congress Hotel with the feeling that, however uncertainly, he had forged the last link in the alliance to keep the nomination from Franklin Roosevelt.

CHAPTER 9

THE DEBACLE
OF THE
TWO-THIRDS RULE

For all his sunny predictions of a first-ballot victory, James Farley knew that, while Roosevelt had a substantial majority of the delegates committed to him, he did not have a two-thirds majority. Farley's predictions were based on the hope that some of the doubtful delegations could be won over before the balloting began and that others would be persuaded by the sheer momentum of the Roosevelt vote to get on the bandwagon. Neither hope was of much comfort to a professional politician such as Farley. He had only to look back to Champ Clark and Martin Van Buren, both of whom were defeated by the two-thirds majority rule even though they had a plurality of the delegates behind them, and to the donnybrook at Madison Square Garden in 1924.

Roosevelt's only certain path to the nomination was for the convention to remove the two-thirds rule and nominate its candidate by a simple majority. This had been done once before, when the Democrats failed to reach a nomination in Charleston, South Carolina, in 1860. On that occasion, the deadlocked delegates adjourned, temporarily suspended the two-thirds rule, reconvened and nominated Stephen Douglas by a simple majority. Douglas was defeated in the November election by Abraham Lincoln, and the Democrats returned to the two-thirds rule thereafter. By 1932, the rule had the force of a century-old party tradition.

Most Democratic politicians resented the rule and felt that it should be permanently eliminated, but a small and aggressive group, concentrated mostly in the Southern states, saw it as a convenient wedge to force the minority will on the conventions, a way to veto unpalatable candidates. Roosevelt and his advisors had foreseen the perils of the two-thirds rule and they also recognized the perils of trying to abrogate it. If he forced the issue on the floor of the convention, Roosevelt ran the risk of losing a lot of his support—again, largely Southern—for the nomination. Like the Walker case, it was a damned-if-he-did and damned-if-he-didn't dilemma. At the high strategy meeting in Hyde Park it had been decided to postpone any decision on the rule until the convention began and its permanent organization was voted on. By that time, it was hoped, the necessary two-thirds majority would be marshalled to the Roosevelt candidacy, and no action on the old rule would be necessary.

The issue surfaced unexpectedly at a meeting of friends of Roosevelt which Farley had intended to be no more than a pep rally. Some 150 people crowded into Roosevelt headquarters just before midnight on the eve of the convention's opening session. At the outset, Farley introduced Bruce Kremer, the chairman-designate of the Rules Committee. Kremer thereupon suggested the desirability of dispensing with the two-thirds majority regulation, and a heated discussion began. Burton Wheeler and Clarence Dill both endorsed the idea, and Huey Long broke in to lash "the financial interests in the East" which were trying to stop Roosevelt. Farley tried vainly to change the subject, but he had lost control of the meeting. Josephus Daniels of North Carolina, who, as the wartime Secretary of Navy, had been Roosevelt's chief, and Cordell Hull of Tennessee urged abrogation, both insisting that no southern votes for Roosevelt would be lost by such action (they proved to be very poor judges of their region).

Huey Long, red-faced, sweating, arms flopping, took the floor again, and proposed a resolution stating that the Roosevelt supporters wanted to scuttle the two-thirds majority rule and substitute a simple majority rule. Then, much to the confusion of his listeners, he asked permission to second his own motion, and launched into a bellowing, rousing speech that enthralled the meeting. When he had finished, his resolution was unanimously adopted by the leaders. Kremer promised to present the resolution to the Rules Committee which, with its large majority of Roosevelt adherents, would undoubtedly approve it and recommend it to the convention.

That night a shaken Farley telephoned Albany to break the news. A thunderstorm had downed telephone wires in New York, and it was several hours before he could get through, compounding his agitation. "The blame was mine for letting the meeting get out of hand," he wrote in his memoir of the convention. He had hesitated to call Long out of order, he explained, because he feared that the temperamental Louisianan might take his delegation—and his considerable influence with other Southern delegations—right out of the Roosevelt fold.*

Roosevelt accepted the news coolly and said that he would go along with the decision of the meeting, even though he had not been consulted. There is evidence that he was privately angry and disturbed by the action. His shocked aides were surprised that he had not been consulted. "We never made a move, large or small, without first consulting him," said Ed Flynn. "We always consulted him." *The New York Times* reported that one of his supporters who attended the meeting called the Governor in Albany and said to him, "Well, we've done it. We're going to beat the two-thirds rule. What do you think about it?" Roosevelt replied, "Why ask me what I think about it? You have done it. Why ask me what I think about it now?"

The next morning, Louis Howe arrived in Chicago and advised Farley not to worry. They could always retreat, he told him, if the issue became too heated. Later in the morning, Farley announced the decision of the meeting to the press and personally presented Long's resolution to the Rules Committee. Later, Farley denied that Roosevelt had been uninformed, or that he had lost control of the meeting. "The action was taken with his knowledge. What we were doing was feeling our way. I was responsible for putting abrogation through the Rules Committee." But other witnesses tell a different story. When Farley lost control of the meeting, Molly Dewson, a Roosevelt campaign worker, reported,"he looked bewildered, confused and pathetic, like a terrier pup who is being reproached for knocking over a vase of flowers."

With the blossoming of Monday afternoon's newspaper headlines, the anti-Roosevelt opposition exploded. Senator Carter Glass, the flinty Virginian, called the move "damaged goods, obtained by a gambler's trick," and demanded the repudiation of any candidate who won the nomination as a

---

* *Although the maverick Long was extremely useful and worked indefatigably for Roosevelt, he bluntly told Ed Flynn that he gave his support only because "he had seen all the other candidates." The shaky Roosevelt-Long alliance was short-lived: within a year Huey Long had turned his back on Roosevelt and was planning the organization of a third party, with himself as Kingfish of the United States. Long's political dreams were ended in a New Orleans hotel by the bullets of an assassin in 1935.*

result of such "irregular proceedings." The three previous Presidential nominees, Smith, Davis, and Cox reacted with a chorus of outraged indignation. "The whole enterprise smacks of poor sportsmanship," thundered Cox. "The two-thirds rule is a tradition of the Democratic Party which has stood for one hundred years," cried Smith. "A new rule should not be adopted in the heat of a political battle. The spirit of American fair play will not tolerate any eleventh-hour, unsportsmanlike attempt to change the rules after the game has been started. This radical change sounds like a cry for the life preservers." From Cleveland, Newton D. Baker chimed in: any nominee under such a suspension of the rules would have "a moral flaw to his title." Alfalfa Bill Murray predicted that, "if the Roosevelt people put it over, it will mean a third party."

It was, reported James Hagerty, the veteran political reporter of *The New York Times,* "the most sensational development in a national convention since 1912."

The Rules Committee met and hammered out a complicated compromise rule in the hope of mollifying at least some of the critics. The two-thirds majority rule would apply until the sixth ballot. If the convention was still deadlocked at that time, the old rule would be dropped, and nomination would be by simple majority. In addition to this rule, the committee added another, which was bound to enrage traditionalists. It would change the convention's order of business, putting the nomination of President and Vice President first on the agenda, before consideration of the party's platform. (Traditionally, the nominations had been the last undertaking of conventions.)

The convention buzzed with talk of the two-thirds majority issue, and little else. All day long, state delegations met in caucus to debate and vote on the issue. Speakers at the opening ceremonies in the Chicago Stadium addressed their words to deaf ears as huddles of delegates gathered all over the hall to discuss the controversial change and its possible effects. Many of the Southern and Western delegations committed to or favoring Roosevelt's candidacy were unalterably opposed to changing the rules. Fistfights broke out in a caucus of the Missouri delegation, and three delegates walked out. Chairman Tom Pendergast followed them into the corridor to rebuke them. New York, with Boss McGooey chairing the caucus, voted 65 to 32 against suspending the two-thirds rule.

The anti-Roosevelt leaders, now provided with a moral issue, continued to belabor the candidate and the proposed change. Smith, learning that the vote had been taken without the knowledge of Roosevelt or the consent of either Roosevelt or Farley, announced that the Governor had lost control of his own organization. "The new generation, Senators Long and Wheeler, have seized the scepter," he claimed. Carter Glass threatened to circulate a petition pledging eminent Democrats to refuse to support or campaign for any nominee who won with less than two-thirds majority. Judge Seabury announced that "any candidate for the presidency who changes the rules . . . cannot, in my judgment, be elected."

Farley, after a sleepless night, was everywhere around the convention on Tuesday morning, consulting his henchmen, eavesdropping on caucuses, watching for any signs of slippage in the delegations. An early-morning nose count indicated that the two-thirds rule would be defeated by 697 to 457 delegate votes. Farley called Albany with this intelligence and then announced that Roosevelt was standing firm on the matter. Almost immediately afterward, Farley began to get reports of defections. Mississippi doggedly stuck to the two-thirds rule in spite of tremendous pressures brought by Long and other Roosevelt spokesmen. In the afternoon, Farley brought twenty North Carolina delegates to his inner sanctum to listen to Roosevelt plead for their votes for abrogation, over his loudspeaker-telephone. They quietly refused and told him they would back the two-thirds rule at all costs.

By late afternoon, the situation was desperate, and the whole Roosevelt organization was coming apart. Farley's delegate count had dropped to 584 for the proposed change, and 565 against it, and the defections were still going on. All over Chicago the word spread that Roosevelt was losing. The implications were ominous indeed: if the convention voted no confidence in the rules change, there would certainly be more defections from the candidate himself. His most sagacious advisors concluded that if he failed to get the two-thirds rule changed, Roosevelt could not possibly muster two-thirds of the delegates to his own nomination, and all of his dreams and careful planning would then go for nothing. The chances of enacting the change were fast waning. And, even if the two-thirds rule were abrogated by a narrow margin and Roosevelt won the nomination by a mere majority, it would be widely regarded as a tainted nomination, with a major split in the Democratic Party an almost inevitable result. Only a few hours before the convention was scheduled to vote on the Rules Committee's recommendations, Farley called Albany with the alarming news. Roosevelt, who had stayed constantly close to an open telephone, promptly agreed to withdraw from his threatened position at once—and as gracefully as possible.

An hour later, reporters were summoned to the Governor's office in Albany. As they filed in, Roosevelt turned off the small radio he had been listening to and picked up a telegram. "Here's something I suppose you will want to get on the wire right away," he said, and read them his telegram to Farley:

THIS IS NO TIME FOR PARTY STRIFE AND MOMENTARY ADVANTAGE. THAT TRUTH BECOMES THE MORE APPARENT WHEN AN HONEST DIFFERENCE OF JUDGMENT IS EXAGGERATED BY THE OPPOSITION PRESS INTO GRAVE INTERNAL DISSENSION. IT IS TO AVOID SUCH AN IMPRESSION THAT I SEND YOU THIS MESSAGE.

THE NEED OF THE NATION—THE NEED OF THE WORLD—IN THESE DISTRESSING DAYS REQUIRES AVOIDANCE OF PERSONAL ANI-MOSITIES AND DISCUSSION OF PROCEDURE, AND CALLS FOR CONCEN-TRATION OF ATTENTION ON PRINCIPLES AND LEADERSHIP . . . I BELIEVE, AND HAVE ALWAYS BELIEVED, THAT THE TWO-THIRDS RULE SHOULD NO LONGER BE ADOPTED. IT IS UNDEMOCRATIC.

NEVERTHELESS, IT IS TRUE THAT THE ISSUE WAS NOT RAISED UNTIL AFTER THE DELEGATES TO THE CONVENTION HAD BEEN SELECTED, AND I DECLINE TO PERMIT EITHER MYSELF OR MY FRIENDS TO BE OPEN TO THE ACCUSATION OF POOR SPORTSMAN-SHIP OR TO THE USE OF METHODS WHICH COULD BE CALLED, EVEN FALSELY, THOSE OF A STEAMROLLER.

I AM ACCORDINGLY ASKING MY FRIENDS IN CHICAGO TO CEASE THEIR ACTIVITIES TO SECURE THE ADOPTION OF A MAJORITY NOMINATING RULE AT THE OPENING OF THE PERMANENT ORGANI-ZATION.

As soon as he received the telegram, Farley raced off to the conference room where the minority members of the Rules Committee all staunch Smith men, were already drafting their minority report, recommending retention of the two-thirds rule. He burst into the conference unannounced, and breathlessly told the startled members, "Look here, just so there won't be any misunderstanding, I want to tell you what our position is. We are for the rules as they now stand and we're for them 1,000 per cent—the two-thirds rule all the way through, and not ending on the sixth ballot or any other ballot."

Bruce Kremer hastily rounded up the full Rules Committee at the stadium and announced that there would be a meeting in the stadium clubroom. But when the committeemen arrived, the Missouri delegation was caucusing in the clubroom. The Missourians mulishly refused to move, and Kremer at first decided to hold the meeting in the corridor. There was little time to lose; the convention would be considering its permanent organization in a matter of minutes. A policeman finally led the committee to a basement lunchroom, where the rules were hastily rewritten, the traditional order of business restored, and the crisis averted. The problem over the two-thirds rule was referred to the 1936 convention, and four years later the principle of simple majority nomination was adopted for all time.

It was a narrow escape from disaster for Roosevelt, and frustrating for his opponents. "We had him licked by seventy-five votes on that proposition," said Murray, through a cloud of smoke. Farley was able to induce the Southern and Western rebels to return the management of the Roosevelt organization to him (Long continued to campaign loudly for abrogation long after it was a dead issue) and order returned, somewhat shakily, to the Roosevelt camp.

The opposition seized on Roosevelt's retreat as another example of his weakness. "The statement is characteristic of him," sneered Hague. "Moreover it confirms my previous charge that he is lacking in loyalty to his friends. He encouraged them to fight the two-thirds rule. Then, when it became apparent that he could not win, he abandoned them all, much to their embarrassment." James Reed added, "The statement revealed to the country what New York and the East know so well, that Mr. Roosevelt cannot stay put on any matter, even where principle is involved."

Many years later James Farley insisted that Roosevelt had indeed been advised that his adherents planned to make their move against the two-thirds rule, and had agreed to it in advance. The story that Roosevelt had not been informed and that he had lost control of the meeting was made up, Farley says, to save face for the Governor. "I went down to the Rules Committee and told Bruce Kremer [that the fight had failed]. Huey was still trying to put it over. Roosevelt had to absolve himself, and I had to take it on the chin."

Although they had lost their moral issue, the leaders of the "Stop Roosevelt" coalition had gained a large point in their struggle, and they now opposed a somewhat tarnished adversary. Some gleefully announced that Roosevelt's chances of winning the nomination had been dashed on the two-thirds majority issue. "They're hanging the millstone around Roosevelt's neck," said John W. Davis cheerfully. "The forces of Smith & The Favorite Sons took fresh heart," reported *Time,* "for if Roosevelt could be stopped, the nominee could be anybody's guess."

CHAPTER 10

THE STRUGGLE OVER THE PERMANENT CHAIRMANSHIP

The retreat from confrontation over the two-thirds rule was a humiliating and costly adventure for Roosevelt and his men, but they faced still another struggle before they reached that moment of political truth, the nominations. The choice of a permanent chairman hung murkily over the convention. A strong, influential and domineering chairman might force the nomination of a candidate on the convention, as Henry Cabot Lodge did in 1920. In many ways—by recognizing certain speakers and refusing to recognize others, by cutting demonstrations short and allowing others to have full play, by conniving with state chairmen and delegation leaders, by applying pressures to delegates with appointive jobs, by packing the galleries with partisans of a favorite candidate—the permanent chairman can exert enormous influence on the course of a convention. At the final strategy meeting at Hyde Park, it had been decided that Senator Tom Walsh should have the job. Walsh could be counted on to steer the convention to any advantage for Roosevelt and to keep a lid on the opposition.

As soon as the name of Walsh was announced as Roosevelt's choice, a week before the convention began, the anti-Roosevelt forces raised the cry of foul play and vacillation once more. Months before, at a meeting of the Democratic National Committee, John Raskob had suggested the name of Jouett Shouse as the official choice for permanent chairman. Such matters are frequently settled at National Committee meetings, and Roosevelt's representatives had offered no objection at the time, so it was assumed that Shouse was acceptable in Albany.

Under normal circumstances, the chairmanship would have been a fitting honorarium for Shouse, who had labored diligently, without pay, with Raskob to keep the Democratic Party alive after the catastrophe of 1928, and to nurse it back to the vigor of 1930, when the House of Representatives was re-won. But Shouse had labored just as diligently to undercut Roosevelt's candidacy. He was at the very heart of the "Stop Roosevelt" movement. He had traveled across the country urging state chairmen to send their delegates to Chicago uninstructed, or pledged to favorite sons. On Raskob's orders, he had refused the request of Charles Michelson, the party's public relations man, to print and distribute the speeches of Roosevelt—something the National Committee would normally do for any candidate. His meddling in the primaries had stirred up enough comment to warrant Roosevelt's angry letter of protest.

There was, however, another reason why Shouse was unacceptable. Although he was a product of the Middle West, he was almost a caricature of a suave, urbane, well-tailored East Coast politician, down to the walking stick, pince-nez, and spats he fancied. He was the image of the fast-talking city slickers who had lifted Al Smith to the titular leadership of the party and plunged it into the disaster of 1928—the type of politician who was deeply distrusted west of the Mississippi and south of the Mason-Dixon Line. Walter Lippmann suggested that Roosevelt was pushed into the struggle over the permanent chairmanship. "A powerful group of his western and southern supporters," Lippmann wrote, "had determined to wipe out as dramatically as possible all vestiges of the Smith-Raskob influence. The fight against Shouse was made in order to obliterate the memories of the campaign of 1928, when those westerners and southerners were compelled at great risk to support Al Smith and to accept John Raskob." In substantiation of Lippmann's reasoning, five of the nine members of Roosevelt's high command who attended the final strategy meeting were Westerners or Southerners, all wounded veterans of 1928, and all insistent that Jouett Shouse should not have the permanent chairmanship.

As soon as Farley announced to the press that the Roosevelt forces would go "down the line" to get the permanent chairman's post for Walsh, Al Smith called fourteen of his closest associates together at a luncheon and announced that they would back Shouse's candidacy "to the last ditch." The word spread that Roosevelt had agreed to accept Shouse months before the convention and had gone back on his word once more. Speaking for the Smith group, James M. Cox said, "The rejection of Mr. Shouse would be nothing short of studied humiliation of a man who has given his time and talents in furtherance of the most essential reorganization of any political party in half a century."

Smith and his allies knew, though, that Shouse could and probably would be rejected by the convention. In this instance, unlike the fight over the two-thirds rule, Farley knew that the votes for Tom Walsh were available, and there was no likelihood of defection. It was the anti-Roosevelt coalition's turn to run for shelter. "A principle is at stake," growled Al Smith, "the principle of keeping your word." Principles or not, Smith sent an emissary to Farley's suite to ask him to withdraw the name of Walsh in return for the withdrawal of Shouse's candidacy, and to substitute McAdoo as permanent chairman, in order to keep the peace and save face. He was told that it was too late.

A group of Kansas delegates called on Farley to ask if they could vote for Shouse and still support Roosevelt. No, snapped Farley—they were pledged to Roosevelt and every cause Roosevelt supported. Shouse was unacceptable because he opposed Roosevelt's candidacy. Anyone who backed Roosevelt must therefore oppose Shouse. There were no further signs of slippage in the Roosevelt ranks.

Inexorably, the matter came to the convention floor. Smith, to the surprise of his followers, took no part in the struggle on Shouse's behalf other than a brief appearance before a caucus of the New York delegation. Instead, he sat flushed and silent, chewing on a cigar, in the midst of his fellow New Yorkers, through all the oratory and the vote. The men of Tammany were so hostile that Farley had trouble finding a seat in the New York delegation section during the balloting.

John Raskob, formally opening the convention, praised his assistant extravagantly and reminded the party that it had paid Shouse "not one penny" for his services, "nor can it compensate him except as it may register its approval and appreciation of his accomplishments" by granting him the chairmanship.

The following day the convention voted. Backing Shouse, John W. Davis led the parade of speakers. He called Shouse "the St. Paul of the Democratic Party," and asked, "Is that vaulting ambition outleaping itself to give him this fleeting honor?" The speeches that followed were strangely muted and apathetic, as if the "Stop Roosevelt" forces had run out of steam.

Delegate Bernice Pyke, a small, white-haired woman from Ohio, was the only speaker who accused Roosevelt of bad faith. Senator Clarence Dill was booed by ardent Smith partisans in the galleries when he inveighed against the "power trust" and accused Smith, Raskob, and Shouse of trying to "rebuke" Walsh.

By a vote of 626 to 528, Tom Walsh was named permanent chairman. A ruggedly handsome, white-haired man, with his acceptance speech jammed into his coat pocket, Walsh walked across the ramp to the platform, with a grim expression on his face, to accept the gavel from Alben Barkley. On the way, he paused to shake the hand of Jouett Shouse. Shouse smiled amiably.

The vote raised the spirits of the Roosevelt camp and helped restore the organization to the solidity it had before the shattering defeat on the two-thirds rule. Two other victories brought even more jubilation to the Congress Hotel headquarters and Albany—the seating of two contested, pro-Roosevelt delegations from Louisiana and Minnesota, by votes of 638¼ to 514¼, and 658¼ to 492¼ respectively. The fact that Roosevelt's strength held as well as it did in the vote for the Louisiana delegation surprised many convention observers, for the delegation was brazenly illegal, composed of Huey Long's hand-picked henchmen, without any consultation with the Louisiana Democratic Committee. F. Scott Lucas of Illinois vigorously protested the seating of the Long delegation, reading a minority report of the Admissions Committee: "Not even a majority of the State Central Committee were present when the delegates were selected for this greatest convention on earth," he protested. "I charge that the methods used in Louisiana were in direct contravention of the principles of the party as laid down by our forefathers. It was dictatorial, illegal and unwarranted, and the party cannot survive if it condones the high-handed practices indulged in in Louisiana." The convention chose to ignore Lucas' evidence and cynically seated Huey Long and his men because they were committed to Roosevelt.

A scrutiny of the vote for permanent chairman gave the Roosevelt forces even more cause for rejoicing. There were small signs of deterioration of the Smith and favorite son strength in several states—two days before the balloting on the nomination was scheduled to begin. In Pennsylvania, an urbanized, eastern state where Al Smith had made a strong showing in the spring primary, and where he claimed thirty-six dedicated delegate votes, the Walsh-Shouse tally showed that he could be sure of only twenty-seven and a half votes.

In Albany, Roosevelt listened to the proceedings with great uneasiness, which was unrelieved by the many long distance telephone calls from aides in Chicago assuring him that Walsh would win. From time to time, the Governor tried to dictate to his two secretaries, Margaret Lehand and Grace Tully, but when the clerk began to call the roll of the states, he gave up any effort to work and concentrated on the radio. When the count was in, Roosevelt beamed at Sam Rosenman, and the tense anxiety which had pervaded the Executive Mansion for two days gave way to jubilation.

"After the Roosevelt victories of today," wrote Arthur Krock, "imaginative persons fancied that they could hear in the near distance the rumble of the bandwagon. Its music was obviously luring delegates from North Carolina and Iowa, and by Thursday, many more may be under its spell."

Maybe. But Howe, Farley, and every knowledgeable politician in Chicago knew that, if the Walsh-Shouse vote was a harbinger of the Presidential nomination itself, the bandwagon still had nearly 150 votes to go in the next two days, and the going would be increasingly rough and steep.

CHAPTER 11

PROHIBITION
AND THE
PLATFORM

On the morning of June 27, the pleasant, balmy weather broke, and Chicago's temperature soared. At the Chicago Stadium, 3,210 delegates, with 1,154 votes to cast, settled into their red undertaker chairs, filling two acres of floor space from wall to wall. (Only 2,326 delegates had attended the Republican Convention.) In the galleries, Mayor Cermak had packed 29,500 spectators, nearly all of them hand-picked supporters of Al Smith, into a space designed to seat 21,000. The sun, blazing through the open windows, filtered through the hundreds of flags on the stadium ceiling, giving the effect of stained glass. Huge kleig lights for the newsreels added to the heat. Air conditioning was almost unknown in 1932, and within half an hour the stadium was like a smoke-filled steam bath. Grover Whelan, New York City's dignified greeter of important visitors, took off his coat for the first time anyone could remember and sat in blue shirtsleeves in the midst of the New York delegation.

Distinguished spectators, beautiful women, famous entertainers, sportsmen, and foreign diplomats, on hand to see the ultimate American spectacle, filled the boxes of the mezzanine. Genevieve Clark Thompson, who had seen her father, Champ Clark, defeated by the two-thirds majority rule in the convention of 1912, had no comment on the impending fight over the controversial rule. Alice Longworth, a member of the Republican side of the Roosevelt family, and no admirer of her distant cousin, explained why she was present: "Obviously I'm here to see the show. I've been going to conventions, both Republican and Democratic, for more than twenty-five years." Mrs. Woodrow Wilson was greeted effusively by Bernard Baruch. Samuel Seabury, a solitary figure, occupied a box directly across the stadium from the speakers' platform. To cut expenses, the Democrats had kept the decorations left behind by the Republicans. George Washington continued to gaze down at the milling throngs from his gold frame.

The press gallery, hovering over the hall, was only half filled when the opening gavel resounded through the stadium. Most of the reporters were elsewhere, covering the heated hearings of the Admissions, Rules, and Resolutions Committees, or trying to keep up with the intensive delegate hunt in the hotels and around the stadium. James Roosevelt, accredited as a convention correspondent for a Boston paper, interviewed Al Smith, and reported, "He's nice. He's always nice."

Albert Ritchie was given an ovation when he took his seat beside the black and orange flag of Maryland. Al Smith entered the stadium after the playing of "The Star Spangled Banner" and made his way, almost unnoticed, to his seat in the New York delegation. The California delegates staged a brief demonstration for the absent John Garner.

At 1 P.M., an hour later than scheduled, John Raskob, a small figure with an almost inaudible voice, called the convention to order. General Evangeline Booth, bonneted and dressed in her uniform as commander of the Salvation Army, gave the opening prayer, making some oblique references to the Eighteenth Amendment ("We must not surrender to the underworld"). Then Raskob delivered a short address, calling for an end to Prohibition and extolling the virtues of Jouett Shouse. Mayor Cermak, a plump man with slicked-back gray hair and the Wilsonian pince-nez that were the mark of a politician of that time, delivered himself of the kind of Chamber of Commerce speech of welcome that conventions must expect of their hosts: "Our city is hopeful that binding friendships and associations will be made, never to be severed, and that each guest coming and going will know us better, love us more, and join in our ambitions to make Chicago ultimately the greatest city in the world."

Alben Barkley, the plump, curly-headed Kentuckian, approached the rostrum, and Raskob turned the gavel over to him. Barkley, a freshman senator, had won the temporary chairmanship of the convention, and the privilege that goes with it of delivering the Keynote Address, because he had yielded the votes of Kentucky to Roosevelt. He was clad in a white linen suit and vest, and his manner was serious, as well it might have been, for the role of temporary chairman is coveted by any politician with ambition, and the Keynote Address sets the whole tone of a convention.

Barkley's address was a good, hard-hitting outline of the nation's problems and the Democratic Party's solutions. It was delivered with such vigor that Barkley's pince-nez bounced off his nose five times in the course of the speech. "No fair man or woman wants to be unjust to Mr. Hoover or his administration," Barkley shouted. "But that the Hoover Administration and the policies it has pursued have largely contributed to the disaster which has overtaken ours and the world's affairs no intelligent observer can dispute."

Barkley advocated lower tariffs as a spur to trade. He called for federal relief for the unemployed and the farmers. His speech was a well-written preview of the platform that the Resolutions Committee was drafting and debating at that moment. When he proposed that the Congress repeal the Eighteenth Amendment and resubmit it to the states for ratification, he touched off a wild demonstration. The galleries, passionately opposed to Prohibition, rang with cheers, and parading, dancing, yelling delegates turned the convention into a melee. Only eight delegations of states where the consumption of alcohol was still considered sinful clung to their standards and sat tight through the demonstration. Fistfights broke out in the delegation from Iowa, where Prohibition was a controversial issue. It was some time before Barkley managed to restore order in the stadium, pounding his gavel and shouting, "Will the convention and the delegation from Iowa come to order!"

The convention and the press liked Barkley and his speech. The next day, when he turned the gavel over to Tom Walsh, he was given an ovation. It was clear that he would go far in the ranks of his party. "This is one keynote speech you can forgive the length," wrote Will Rogers, "for when you jot down our ills, you got to have a lot of paper. He had it all over the Republican keynoter, for this fellow was reading the facts, while the other fellow had to read alibis."

The search for delegates, the offering of bribes, the bargaining for support, intensified on the floor of the convention, in secret conference rooms, and on the telephone, and the anger and bitterness of the opposing candidates grew. The air of Chicago was blue with charges of foul play, with claims and counterclaims of delegate backing, with rumors and defamation of character. On the day before the convention opened, J. Hamilton Lewis sent a telegram to the Illinois delegation, saying that Senate business kept him in Washington, and releasing his supporters. It was the first breach in the ranks of the favorite sons. Emissaries from Smith, Roosevelt, and Ritchie ran like chickens at mealtime to find out how many votes they could pick up. They were disappointed when Mayor Cermak switched Cook County's bloc of delegates to Melvin Traylor, to be held in reserve for Anton Cermak's political advantage.

When he was not coping with the crisis over the two-thirds rule, James Farley was busy seeking delegates from Texas and California. Looking for Sam Rayburn, he encountered Silliman Evans, the Texas newspaperman (later the publisher of the Chicago *Sun* and owner of the Nashville *Tennessean*), and asked him to arrange a meeting. Evans was a close friend of Garner and Rayburn, and he agreed to see what he could do. Late that night, after eleven P.M., the two Texans came to Farley's suite. Farley and his wife were alone. The three men retired to the bedroom, and Farley gave Rayburn his most vigorous sales pitch. He said that Roosevelt had the most votes, that he was entitled to win by virtue of his long lead over all of the other candidates, and he asked Rayburn to persuade the Speaker to release his votes to Roosevelt as the shortest route to a two-thirds majority. Then he offered the Vice-Presidential nomination to Garner as a final lure.

Rayburn listened attentively, without comment, until Farley had finished. Then he began to talk, slowly in his Texas drawl: "We have come here to Chicago to nominate Speaker Jack Garner for the Presidency if we can. We are not against any other candidate, and we are not for any other candidate. Governor Roosevelt is the leading candidate, and naturally he must be headed off if we are to win. But we don't intend to make it another Madison Square Garden."

That was all. There were no promises, no unspoken understanding, just a hint. The three men agreed to keep their meeting a secret, informing only Roosevelt and Howe. Farley, elated over what he thought were the implications of Rayburn's statement, sprinted off to tell Howe all about it. Howe was unimpressed. There was no point in pursuing Texas and California, he felt. It was just a waste of Farley's time. Howe was concentrating on Harry Byrd and Virginia's twenty-six votes. He spent his days conferring, never leaving the hotel, constantly telephoning. "No one would ever believe how many delegates we won by a telephone call," said Farley.

Both men were exhausted from their efforts, and dispirited by their lack of success. Howe, especially, was physically ill, and the pain he felt was mirrored in his lined, pitted face. He weighed less than one hundred pounds, suffered a heart ailment, and was wracked by asthma, which was not helped by the torrid heat or by his chain smoking. Farley's ebullience ebbed away under Howe's mood of depression. "The unbearable pressure of the past few days was beginning to have its effect, and we knew it," Farley recalled in his memoirs. "The struggle for delegates had become so intense that honest rivalry was giving way to bitterness and ugly feeling."

Howe and Farley quarreled over the sensibility of negotiating with the Texans. It was the first disagreement the two had had on a question of strategy, and they finally telephoned Albany for instructions. Roosevelt listened to his two deputies, then told them to go on negotiating in both directions—Farley to continue putting pressure on Rayburn, and Howe to keep after Byrd.

The following day, Farley cornered Rayburn and Evans again, in the back room of Garner headquarters. He implored them to cast Texas' votes for Garner on the first ballot and then, having shown their loyalty to the Speaker for the record, to switch to Roosevelt at the end of the balloting. Mister Sam asked Farley how long he thought he could sustain Roosevelt's voting strength without deterioration. "Three ballots, four ballots, maybe five," said Farley. "Well," said Rayburn, "we just must let the convention go for a while, even if we are interested in the Vice Presidency—and I'm not saying we are." It was just another hint, a broader hint, perhaps, but it boosted Farley's hopes again.

On Tuesday morning, the newspapers revealed the existence of Newton Baker's secret recruiting post at the Congress. The convention was immediately swept with rumors about Baker's rising strength. He had nine and a half of Mississippi's delegates in hand, and it was reported that he was making serious inroads on nearly every other southern and western delegation. According to some news reports, Baker had cornered more than one hundred votes.

The news alarmed the forward observers of William Randolph Hearst who were at the convention. Damon Runyon, one of Hearst's most famous writers, brought Colonel Joseph Willicombe, Hearst's confidential secretary, to see Farley. The three conferred, warily and worriedly, then decided to telephone "The Chief" in California. Hearst listened as each of the three men in turn told him the news about Newton Baker and assured him that, if Roosevelt lost the nomination, it would almost certainly go to Baker. Hearst, who had thought that the worst candidate he could expect after a Roosevelt defeat would be Albert Ritchie, was alarmed and furious. He refused, however, to use his influence on the California delegation.

News of a possible deadlock filtered back to Washington, and two Senators, Harry B. Hawes of Missouri and Key Pittman of Nevada, decided to take some unilateral action. Hawes supported Roosevelt and Pittman favored Garner and both had heard rumors that the Speaker might be agreeable to release his delegates if the Vice Presidency was offered to him.

Hawes called Roosevelt in Albany, explained his distress over the possibility of a convention deadlock, and asked if Garner would be an acceptable running mate. If Roosevelt agreed, Hawes was willing to appeal to Garner, who, he knew, was also very much opposed to another Madison Square Garden situation. Roosevelt was enthusiastic. "Senator, that would be fine," he said, "the Governor from New York and the Speaker of the House from Texas. Clear across the country." He told Hawes to notify Farley.

Hawes immediately sent a telegram to Chicago:

GROUP HERE BELIEVE WINNING TICKET WOULD BE ROOSEVELT AND GARNER STOP NINETY VOTES OF CALIFORNIA AND TEXAS WOULD ELIMINATE DISPUTE STOP AM ADVISED WOULD BE SATISFACTORY TO PARTY HERE STOP SEE SAM RAYBURN TOM CONNALLY AND CHECK MY OWN IMPRESSION STOP BEST WISHES.

Along with this message, Hawes and Pittman sent hundreds of other telegrams to delegates in Chicago and political leaders around the country, urging support of a Roosevelt-Garner ticket.

Hawes and Pittman acted without consulting Garner, and merely assumed he was available for the Vice Presidency. They were wrong. When Garner awoke the next morning, he was bombarded with inquiries and reports of the Hawes-Pittman campaign. Red with rage, he telephoned Hawes and excoriated him. He had no wish to be Vice President, he said, his voice shrill with anger. It was a meaningless post. It was "not worth a cup of warm spit." No one but Sam Rayburn had the right to act or speak for him. Hawes called on Garner in his office later in the day to apologize, and managed to soothe his ruffled feelings.

The convention rolled on, sweltering in the savage heat wave from the prairies. The Resolutions Committee considered hundreds of proposed planks for the platform. A suggestion to include a Free Armenia resolution was turned down. Bishop Cannon turned up again to lobby for Prohibition and was startled when a delegate handed him a bottle of bay rum and photographers took his picture. His brow darkened with episcopal rage, and he threatened to smash the bottle and the cameras.

Robert K. Hutchins, the "boy wonder" president of the University of Chicago, impressed the committee with a fervent plea for youth to be heard:

I believe the Democratic Party has the greatest opportunity of its career to enlist under its banner the younger generation of this nation [he said], but it must state in unequivocal terms its position on some of the fundamental problems of today.

If you do not, a youth movement will arise throughout this country that will express itself through the formation of a third party. The Republican platform brings no response from our hearts, and we cannot follow you unless you stand for the principles we stand for.

When he had finished, young Dr. Hutchins was wildly applauded. McAdoo and A. Mitchell Palmer, both members of the committee, rushed to shake his hand. Later, before a group of four hundred Young Democrats, Hutchins presented a "platform for youth" that was much admired. At a press conference, Farley mentioned Hutchins and Barkley as promising Vice Presidential candidates—but not Garner, or any of the favorite sons.

Huey Long called Roosevelt in Albany and asked him to urge the Resolutions Committee to put a plank in the platform asking for immediate payment of a bonus to veterans of World War I. Roosevelt refused, saying he was against bonuses as a matter of principle. "Well, you are a gone goose," said Long.

In the committee there was heated debate over the question of federal aid to the unemployed. "It would be a damnable outrage bordering on treason," said Cordell Hull, "if this Democratic Convention, like the recent Republican Convention, should meet and adjourn without any serious thought or mention of the unprecedented crisis." Any delegates who wanted to skirt the issue, he added, should be thrown into Lake Michigan.

The stickiest problem facing the Resolutions Committee was Prohibition. Two thirds of the committee members insisted on an ultra-wet resolution, asking Congress to repeal the Eighteenth Amendment, and one third held out for a more moderate approach, referring the question to the state legislatures for a decision. A minority report, and a divisive debate on the convention floor, like the Republican fight over Prohibition, seemed inevitable. The struggle spread to the delegations. Among the Texans it was a question of upholding Prohibition, which was very close to being an article of their fundamentalist faith, or backing John Garner, who had advocated Repeal in his effort to attract Northern and Midwestern votes. A Texas caucus in a room just off the floor of the convention became so heated that more fistfights broke out among the delegates. When a policeman offered to intervene to restore peace, he was pushed out of the room and told, "This is a private fight. Get out!"

There was tension in the Roosevelt ranks as reports came to Farley's suite that signs of slippage had appeared in many delegations. Four Minnesota delegates out of twenty-four were ready to switch to Baker. Mississippi seethed with unrest. Both Illinois and Indiana were reported moving toward Al Smith, but Smith had to remain aloof in order to keep the favorite sons from suspecting his real ambitions, and could do nothing personally to encourage them. To the press, Farley exuded confidence, although he retreated slightly from his flat preconvention prediction, "I tell you, it's Roosevelt on the first ballot." Now, he said that Roosevelt could count on 690 to 700 votes. "We hope there will be sufficient shifts to give him two thirds and bring about his nomination on the first ballot."

"How is New York going to vote?" a reporter asked.

"I don't know about New York," Farley replied, "but I hope for the best."

"How about the reports that Roosevelt is losing votes in Mississippi, Iowa, West Virginia, and Alabama?"

Farley was confident: "There is no danger there."

The opposition was just as serene. Mayor Hague announced that the opponents of Roosevelt had five hundred or more first-ballot votes, undoubtedly held the veto power over the Roosevelt candidacy, and would hold on as long as those states uncommitted to Roosevelt stayed firmly with their candidates:

> I think there is ground for reliance that, with the better leadership in the organizations from the important states which so far are not in the Roosevelt column, there will be concert of action up to the point where Mr. Roosevelt will be forced to quit. Unless there is a bandwagon rush on the first or second ballot, in my opinion, the Roosevelt bloc is sunk. They will never be able to put over their candidate after the third ballot in this convention.

Smith's personal strength was reckoned at two hundred ballots, all but twenty-one from five Eastern states.

Charges of foul play and the use of bribery were heard on all sides. An Iowa delegate told Louis Howe that he had been awakened at 4 A.M. by an anonymous telephone caller, who wanted to know how many ballots he intended to vote for Roosevelt. Delegate William McMasters of Boston, a Smith supporter, denied that he had offered ten thousand dollars to Frank Schofield, campaign manager for Melvin Traylor, to withdraw Traylor as a candidate. "All I suggested, as a lifelong Democrat, was that Mr. Traylor release the delegates committed to him," he explained. Traylor himself was unable to appear personally at the convention. A run on his bank kept him hard at work.

Farley grasped at every straw. When a group of delegates came to him to find out how close the Roosevelt vote count was to a two-thirds majority, he noted with satisfaction that four of them were from Missouri, and interpreted this as an indication of a possible shift of ballots away from favorite son James Reed. Farley and Howe were both pleased to note a sudden change of editorial policy in the Hearst papers, with the appearance of friendly articles about Roosevelt.

Farley, Howe, and Hague spent another night without sleep, keeping a constant watch over their delegations. At dawn a kilted band of Oklahoma schoolgirls serenaded Governor Murray in front of the hotel, which might have cost him the votes of friendly delegates who wanted to sleep. Al Smith worked diligently in the daytime, lunching on hot dogs at the stadium and presiding over enormous press conferences. He found time to play a round of golf every afternoon, though, and made the tactical blunder of appearing at the convention one night in evening clothes. Jimmie Walker was conspicuously absent from the convention floor. He attended the races with Vincent Bendix and John D. Hertz, the owner of a taxicab fleet, and was seen at a party at the Edgewater Beach Hotel.

The convention unanimously approved the revised rules, and voted Thomas Walsh in as permanent chairman. Missouri cast 29½ votes for Walsh, confirming Farley's speculation that the delegates' support of Reed was faltering, but this gain for Roosevelt was offset by the loss of six Alaskan delegates and seven out of the twelve-man delegation from Maine, who voted for Jouett Shouse.

With the Resolutions Committee still wrestling with the Prohibition issue, the convention found itself with nothing to do, and a parade of entertainers and celebrities took over the speakers' rostrum. Walsh turned over the gavel to Eddie Dowling, the song-and-dance man, who introduced Amos and Andy, the radio comedians; Gene Tunney, the retired heavyweight champion; Father Coughlin; Grace Bryan Hargreaves, the daughter of William Jennings Bryan; Clarence Darrow; and the Columbus, Ohio, Glee Club, who sang the "Main Stein Song," perhaps in anticipation of the Prohibition resolution. "As soon as enough members of the committee get sober, we probably will hear the prohibition plank," Will Rogers told the delegates.

The convention recessed for dinner and agreed to meet again at 7 P.M. when the Resolutions Committee would have its report ready. By late afternoon the committee finished its labors in the sumptuous splendors of the Rose Room of the Congress and brought forth a majority report, asking Congress to repeal the Eighteenth Amendment and quickly legalize beer, and a more moderate minority report, urging resubmission of the Prohibition issue to the states. The Committee's vote on the question of Repeal was 35–17.

Walsh gaveled the convention to order at seven fifty—late as usual, in the best tradition of Democratic conventions. Every seat was occupied, and there was an air of tense expectancy that lasted through the four-hour debate. There was confusion on the floor, and when Walsh ordered the aisles cleared, an enormous demonstration began. Walter Denegre, a delegate from Washington, D.C., led the parade of wet states, singing the "Stein Song," "How Dry I Am," and "Sweet Adeline." Only seven delegations remained in their seats. A delegate from Delaware seized the Virginia standard and carried it into the throng. The Crusaders, the repeal group, unfurled a banner with the slogan, "End Prohibition," and joined the demonstration. An estimated 24,000 people participated, dancing, singing, waving steins and beer bottles. Women in the galleries waggled their fingers, which were adorned with thimbles—the emblem, for some strange reason, of a women's repeal organization. Walsh, an abstainer, watched the demonstration coldly and was finally, after fifteen minutes, able to restore order. But a fight started in the Texas delegation, still bitterly divided by the issue of Demon Rum, and Colonel Edwin A. Halsey, sergeant-at-arms of the convention, had to call in reinforcements from his guards to calm the Texans down. As Cordell Hull took the stand to defend the minority report, the Texas delegates left their seats and filed out of the stadium to hold yet another caucus. When they returned, they had cast their lot with the majority report and John Garner.

Three Presidential candidates took part in the debate—Smith and Ritchie, speaking for the Wet resolution, and Murray, defending the Dry position. When Al Smith mounted the rostrum, in his only appearance there during the convention, he was greeted by a roaring, ten-minute ovation from the galleries and a milling demonstration on the floor. His face was flushed, his collar drenched, and he drank three glasses of water as he waited for order to be restored. He was an older Al Smith, thicker in the waistline, with whiter hair and deeper lines in his face, but the crowd in the galleries still loved him. Not everyone in the stadium was applauding him—portraits of Roosevelt and Garner were hoisted in the Nebraska delegation—and he must have had some feeling that this might be his last appearance on the national stage. If so, he gave his listeners their money's worth, with a stem-winding, up-from-the-floor attack on the Eighteenth Amendment, delivered in the classic Al Smith style, from jottings on an envelope. The spectators in the galleries cheered him wildly.

Some of the elders at the stadium felt that the Repeal resolution went too far, that Congress would never enact such a law, and that it would be better simply to resubmit the question to the states. "It's a barroom plank," complained Carter Glass, a teetotaler. "It's too wet," said John Raskob, who had urged the party to take a stand for Repeal in his opening address to the convention. But in the end, the delegates voted jubilantly for the plank, 934¾ to 213¾. Only Alabama, Arkansas, Georgia, Kansas, Mississippi, and Oklahoma voted Dry. "The Democratic South has been the chief factor in enacting national prohibition," wrote Arthur Krock. "In voting that it should be repealed, Democracy, like Saturn, was swallowing its own child."

The clamor over Prohibition disturbed John Dewey, the philosopher and teacher, who was an interested observer at the convention. "Here we are, in the midst of the greatest crisis since the Civil War," he said, "and the only thing the two national parties seem to want to debate is booze."

H. L. Mencken, one of the loudest advocates of Repeal, was delighted with the resolution, but he foresaw trouble ahead for the Democrats in the "Bible Belt." Delegates from the South and Midwest, he wrote, will be "going home with a tattered Bible on one shoulder and a shiny beer seidel on the other, and what they will have to listen to from their pastors and the ladies of the W.C.T.U. is making their hearts miss every other beat."

There was no quarrel with the rest of the platform, a seventeen-point document set forth in a terse 1,450 words, the briefest in history. Its economic resolutions, written by Cordell Hull, were extremely conservative, and were never, really, to be fulfilled. The platform proposed the reduction of appropriations for the operation of the federal government by 25 per cent, a balanced budget governed by "a system of taxation levied on the principle of ability to pay," and an international silver conference. Other resolutions had a very liberal ring and were the harbingers of such innovations to come as the Securities and Exchange Commission, the N.R.A., and government work projects. Federal credit to the states for the relief of the unemployed was proposed, along with "a federal program of necessary and useful construction," and "a substantial reduction of the hours of labor." The financial community got a nasty rap in a recommendation, written by Senator Glass, of government regulation of holding companies and the separation of banks and affiliated investment companies, along with "protection of the investing public by requiring to be filed with the government and carried in advertisements of all offerings of stocks and bonds, true information as to bonuses, commissions, principal invested and interests of sellers."

The nation's farmers got a pat on the head with promises of "better financing of farm mortgages . . . at low rates of interest . . . effective control

of crop surpluses . . . every Constitutional measure that will aid the farmer."
The issue of a veterans' bonus was skirted ("the fullest measure of justice
and generosity") and the proposed cancellation of the European war debts
was firmly opposed. Independence for the Philippines was advocated, and
ultimate statehood for Puerto Rico.

The Republicans were given a severe drubbing in the platform's
preamble:

> In this time of unprecedented economic and social distress the Demo-
> cratic Party declares its conviction that the chief causes of this condition
> were the disastrous policies pursued by our government since the
> World War . . . Those responsible have ruined our foreign trade,
> destroyed the values of our commodities and products, crippled our
> banking system, robbed millions of their life savings and thrown mil-
> lions more out of work, produced widespread poverty and brought the
> Government to a state of financial distress unprecedented in time of
> peace . . . The only hope lies in a drastic change.

McAdoo had a bank deposit guarantee plank, and Murray offered a
complete substitute platform, which included a bonus for veterans, but both
were rejected, along with all of the other minority reports except one—a
single sentence pledging a Democratic administration to continued concern
for child welfare—offered by Mrs. Caroline O'Day of New York, a close
friend of Eleanor Roosevelt. The convention adopted the entire platform
in one whooping "Aye," without a single dissent. It was a statement tailored
to Franklin Roosevelt's wishes—crisp, ringing, brief—and it brought a
feeling of exhilaration to Albany, for it was almost precisely the same document that Mitchell Palmer and Cordell Hull had prepared in Washington.

In Albany, Roosevelt fired off a telegram to Farley:

THE COUNTRY AND THE PARTY OUGHT TO BE CONGRATULATED ON
THE SHORTEST, CLEAREST, AND MOST READABLE PLATFORM IN OUR
WHOLE HISTORY . . . I AM FOR IT.

The convention adjourned at midnight, to resume its deliberations at
1 P.M. the following afternoon and take up the question of nominating a
Presidential candidate.

CHAPTER 12

DEADLOCK

The struggle for delegates continued through the night and into the morning. Roosevelt's managers concentrated on the delegations of New York, Illinois, Mississippi, and Oklahoma. The anti-Roosevelt forces put pressure on the delegations of Indiana, Mississippi, Iowa, Minnesota, and Alabama, where many delegates with strong anti-Roosevelt sentiments chafed at the unit rule. Every one of the five delegations, with a total of 124 votes, had figured in Farley's predictions.

Al Smith and John W. Davis visited the Mississippi delegation in the morning to argue on behalf of Newton Baker. After they left, the delegation caucused and found a substantial majority were for Baker. At that point Huey Long, in a rumpled pongee suit, hurried in to talk the Mississippians out of their rebellion. After a half-hour tirade, with Long using every dramatic trick in his repertoire, the delegation voted again, and, very shakily, returned to the Roosevelt ranks. Frank Hague claimed that anti-Roosevelt candidates had gained three and a half votes and control of the Iowa delegation.

Arthur Brisbane, on orders from Hearst, began direct negotiations with Sam Rayburn in an attempt to get Garner to swing the Texas-California bloc behind Albert Ritchie. Rayburn refused. Ritchie had only twenty-one Maryland votes to begin with, he explained, and was too risky to rely on. Such a switch might easily lead to a chaotic scramble for delegates and throw the nomination to Baker or some other dark horse.

James Curley, at Farley's request, telephoned Hearst at his San

Simeon home, to raise the specter of Newton Baker once more. The publisher still refused to come to the support of Roosevelt. John F. Curry, who had deliberately postponed a caucus of the New York delegation in order to keep Roosevelt's managers guessing, finally called for a vote. Jimmie Walker told his colleagues to forget about the Seabury charges and vote according to their sentiments. A suggestion that the uncommitted votes be divided among out-of-state candidates was considered and dropped. In the caucus, the New Yorkers split, casting sixty-five votes for Smith, twenty-eight and a half for Roosevelt.

Before the nominations began, word reached the press gallery that Al Smith was going to withdraw his candidacy and release his delegates to vote as they pleased. The rumor was attributed to Farley. Smith, infuriated, announced that he was going to confront Farley with the report and demand an explanation. But Farley denied any part in spreading the story before Smith could reach him. Smith told a press conference,

> I am not only going to stick, I am going to be nominated. I have spent a large part of my career with newspapermen. I found them always to be fair. I wish I could say as much about the adherents of one of the candidates, who today have been passing the word around that I am withdrawing, or that I concede the nomination of anyone on the second, third or any other ballot.
>
> Nothing is to be gained by small tactics or mean plays in a big game. This line of information is designed to deceive the whole country. The enthusiasm for a cause has deadened their sense of fair play.

Hague also denounced the rumor mongers and reiterated his claim that Roosevelt was a weak candidate who could not win. Roosevelt's record-breaking plurality in 1930, he said, was the result of Republican unhappiness over the Prohibition issue and a consequent failure of Republicans to vote in New York State.

A reporter asked Sam Rayburn if he had been offered the Vice Presidency for John Garner. "Yes I have," he said, "and we minced no words in declining to consider the proposal." Just before the convention met to begin the nominations, Farley told reporters that he had raised his first-ballot prediction for the Roosevelt tally from 691 to 705 votes, "depending on the maturity of some reflections now in the minds of certain gentlemen."

When Tom Walsh gaveled for order, the floor of the convention was a scene of pandemonium, as campaign managers and their scouts prowled the arena, looking everywhere for stray votes. The strain had reached an almost unbearable peak, and there was great bitterness in the Roosevelt and

Smith camps. The bushy head of Arthur Mullen, Roosevelt's floor manager, was conspicuous in the milling crowd, as he moved from delegation to delegation, checking the battle lines. Frank Hague, in his stiff collar, looked "almost as concerned as he did when the New Jersey legislature cited him for contempt," said *The New York Times.* To Raymond Daniell, the scene resembled the New York Stock Exchange on a busy afternoon. "The center aisle in front of the Speakers' platform was full of traders all day long. The bidding and asking in the vicinity of the New York and New Jersey standards was as active as any that took place around the Montgomery-Ward and General Motors posts in the good old days."

Walsh managed to bring the convention to order of a sort, and Reading Clerk Patrick J. Haltigan began to call the roll of the states in a stentorian baritone. For five hours the conventioneers listened to nominating and seconding speeches and cavorted in lengthy demonstrations for each candidate, then adjourned for three hours, followed by six more hours of oratory and demonstrations. It was after four in the morning and the dawn was breaking over Lake Michigan before the first ballot was cast. Farley and Howe had rigorously trimmed Roosevelt's seconding speeches and sought in other ways to hasten the balloting, but the opposition deliberately protracted its oratory and demonstrations in the hope of winning time and postponing a vote for another day.

The demonstrations alone, as stop-watched by *Time,* consumed four hours and four minutes, from 62 minutes for Al Smith to four minutes for Governor White. The speeches for the nine candidates—some of them quite ordinary men—depicted a pantheon of gods. A sampling:

John E. Mack: "Country born and country living, this man's whole political life is an open book. His reputation is unsullied, his character spotless. Has there ever been a breath of suspicion against him? . . . The candidate of this convention shall be, must be and will be FRANKLIN DELANO ROOSEVELT!"

Tom Connally: "The man whom I present to this convention has spent his life among the people of his own country. Reared in humble surroundings, he has risen to a place of power . . . I present as the field marshal of the armies of Democracy the great Speaker of the House, JOHN NANCE GARNER!"

Joseph Ely: "The great constitutional lawyers of his day acknowledge his divine gift of government . . . The savior of his nation, this positive, virile, straight-speaking statesman . . . For the Democratic Party, for the United States of America, for the needs of humanity, I give to this convention the name of ALFRED E. SMITH!"

And so it went. Harry Byrd, said Carter Glass, "united the gracious manners of a gentleman with the fine virtues of a yeoman." Ritchie was "this matchless master of the art of government." Murray was the "God-gifted, gigantic leader of the Party." Through the long night, more than fifty speakers extolled the virtues of these paragons of politics. When Louisiana was called, Huey Long barked, "Loosiana yields in the hope of putting an end to all these useless seconding speeches." It was a forlorn hope; the oratorical parade rumbled on. Nor were the speeches uninterrupted. Mack's voice was drowned out three times by boos from the hostile galleries, and Walsh had to intervene to restore order. When Homer Cummings came to the rostrum to second Roosevelt's nomination, a belligerent delegate, David E. Fitzgerald, protested, "The Connecticut delegation was instructed by the state convention that elected it to vote for Governor Alfred E. Smith. Mr. Cummings has no right——." Chairman Walsh rapped briskly for order in the booing, groaning galleries and ruled that Cummings, as an individual, could speak. Representative John E. Rankin of Mississippi, endorsing Roosevelt, said, "I hope the people who are listening in realize that those jeers are coming from the galleries and not from the delegates." There were no objections to the seconding speeches for Smith, all of them delivered by captive supporters from delegations pledged by the unit rule to Roosevelt.

Al Smith arrived at the stadium just as the nominating speeches began and headed for the speakers' platform. As he started across the ramp, he heard Roosevelt's name mentioned. He stopped short and his face darkened. "Hell, I can listen to that at the hotel," he muttered, and returned to his own headquarters, where he listened to Mack's nominating speech without comment. Then he retired to his suite where he heard his own nomination in seclusion. Later, he told reporters that Ely's tribute was "the best speech I have ever heard in any convention since the days of Bourke Cockran." Cockran was a golden-voiced New York congressman who nominated Smith for the Presidency in 1920, a year when he had no serious Presidential ambitions. Smith's statement was, of course, a slap at the man who had twice nominated him in 1924 and 1928 and dubbed him "The Happy Warrior."

In Albany, Roosevelt, surrounded by his family and friends, said of Mack's rather lackluster, poorly delivered speech, "It was fine, it was great!" and fired off another telegram:

MY AFFECTIONATE THANKS TO YOU, MY OLD FRIEND, FOR THAT FINE SPEECH. NO MATTER WHAT THE RESULTS TODAY, YOU AND I WILL ALWAYS GO ON TOGETHER.

In Washington John Garner, who had not turned a radio on since the convention began, continued to turn a deaf ear to the events in Chicago. When the delegates were reassembling after their dinner break, at 9:30 P.M., the Speaker was in bed.

The demonstrations followed the traditional cue, "Gentleman, I give you . . ." and provided the convention with some respite from the purple oratory. When Mack reached his peroration, the delegates were too busy attaching pictures of Roosevelt to their standards and the sticks of new brooms to listen to him. As a giant portrait of Roosevelt unfurled from the galleries, Al Melgard, the stadium organist, who had only nine fingers, pulled all 883 stops and filled the stadium with a mighty blast of "Anchors Aweigh." To Louis Howe, wracked with asthma in his hotel room, it sounded more like a dirge than a victory anthem. It was one detail he had overlooked. He reached for the telephone and called Ed Flynn at the stadium. "For God's sake, tell 'em to play something else," he said, between coughing fits. "Tell 'em, oh, tell 'em to play 'Happy Days Are Here Again.'" Melgard quickly changed his tune and launched into the song that would be identified with Roosevelt for the rest of his life.

On the floor, the convention turned into a vast melee. Jimmy Roosevelt raced down the aisle like a schoolboy and snatched the New York standard next to John Curry, who remained seated. His brother, Franklin, Jr., scrambled over the side of a box and joined him. Two Warm Springs delegates carried a large, home-made placard that read:

> The Ship of State is going past,
> There is no captain at the mast,
> Time has come your votes to cast,
> And put a captain at the mast!
> ROOSEVELT

In his hotel room, Al Smith snorted. The captain should be at the bridge, he said, not at the mast.

A strange banner, held by a New Yorker, read, "New York's delegates are loyal to you and will see that you come true." Georgians threw serpentine. A girl in white rode piggy-back on the back of a Nebraska delegate. Farley, wearing a ten-gallon hat and looking sheepish, observed it all from the speakers' platform. The demonstration faltered, then revived again when a busty matron pushed her way through the crowd on the rostrum to the microphone and sang "Ioway." Looking very grim, Walsh finally succeeded in halting the demonstration after forty-three minutes.

When Tom Connally nominated Garner, one thousand marchers,

led by the imported "Old Gray Mare Band" whooped it up for half an hour, to the tune of "Dixie." McAdoo, flanked by two pretty girls, cakewalked down the aisle. The Richmond Light Infantry Blues, in their plumed kepis and War of 1812 uniforms, led the demonstration for Harry Byrd. Debutante Margaret Penfield waved the Old Dominion flag from the rostrum, and a covey of frightened doves was released. The bass drum in the band was supported by a stooped Negro. In the parade for Ritchie, a black-haired beauty, Mrs. W. W. Lenahan, waved the Maryland standard and lured delegates to join the demonstration. When she blew Huey Long a kiss, he stepped in line.

The largest and longest demonstration was for Al Smith, and, for the first and only time, the spectators in the galleries participated, waving placards and flags, and showering the hall with confetti. Daniell reported seeing a stout lady in the balcony above the rostrum who took the straw hat of the man next to her, smashed the top in, replaced the brim on his head and handed the top to him. He calmly sailed it down over the heads of the frolicking demonstrators. A quartet who took possession of the platform, gave the demonstration a properly boozy atmosphere, singing "How Dry I Am" and "Sweet Adeline," while other demonstrators waved glasses, steins, and brown jugs. After more than an hour, the demonstration came to an exhausted end.

The last hurrah was not heard until after four in the morning, and many of the weary delegates wanted to go to bed. Many had already collapsed from exhaustion and the heat: the stadium hospital reported twenty-two patients, suffering from heat prostration or stomach disorders. There might have been more, but for a fortuitous thunderstorm that broke at three in the morning and brought the temperature down twenty degrees. Andy Frain's ushers flung the stadium doors and windows open, and the place was comfortably cool for a few hours. By the time the demonstrations ended, the big arena was a shambles. John W. Davis and many other delegates slept in their chairs. Half the audience had departed, and there were large sections of empty chairs among the delegations.

From the beginning, the Roosevelt strategy had been to press for a vote, no matter how late the hour, and try for a quick, first-ballot victory. The anti-Roosevelt strategy was just the opposite—to prolong the proceedings and force the convention to adjourn before taking a vote.

In the early hours of the morning, Farley retired to his tiny conference room, stretched out on a cot, and called a meeting of his lieutenants. All agreed that the balloting should proceed without delay, no matter how late the hour. Farley telephoned Roosevelt at the Executive Mansion in Albany, and got an official green light; the Roosevelt family was prepared to sit up all night. All of the friendly chairmen were thereupon notified to keep their delegates at the stadium and to be ready to ballot, no matter how late.

At the end of the nominations, two efforts were made by Tom Connally to adjourn the convention. The vote on the first motion, by voice, was inconclusive, but a roll-call vote showed that only four of the anti-Roosevelt states—New York, California, Texas, and Oklahoma—wanted adjournment. Frank Hague had decided to go along with the balloting; enough votes were available, he was certain, to force a stalemate in the first ballot. Hague announced that he wanted as many ballots as the Roosevelt partisans desired. Al Smith returned to the stadium, on Hague's insistence, and began holding conferences with delegates.

At 4:28 A.M., Chairman Walsh ordered the clerk to call the roll of the states. Again, the "Stop Roosevelt" forces used the tactics of delay. The roll call took nearly three hours to complete. In the midst of the balloting, Minnesota's delegation produced a telegram from the state Democratic Committee, releasing the delegation from its commitment to Roosevelt. In the uproar that followed the announcement, Walsh ruled that the telegram was without authority. All twenty-four of the Minnesotans cast their votes for Roosevelt as a unit. Walsh then asked that the delegation be polled. If two thirds of the Minnesotans agreed to release their votes, he ruled, then they could vote as they wished on subsequent ballots. The poll was taken and the Minnesota delegation voted for retention of the unit rule.

It was a near thing for Roosevelt, for under Jouett Shouse or some other unfriendly chairman, the episode would almost certainly have started a breakdown of the Roosevelt machinery, with Mississippi and other mutinous states demanding an end to unit rule, too.

When the roll call reached New York there was another lengthy delay. Curry demanded a poll of the delegation. There was no reason for it; Roosevelt's partisans within the delegation had no quarrel with Curry's tabulation of their votes. It was simply another means of prolonging the ordeal. It also gave Jimmie Walker an opportunity to make a grandstand play. Walker entered the hall unobserved, late in the polling, and asked to be heard. Walsh asked,

> Who is the gentleman who addresses the chair?
> Walker, a delegate from New York.
> For what purpose does he address the chair?
> The delegate was not here when his name was called, and his alternate voted in his stead. The delegate is now here and requests permission to cast his own vote.

The request is granted.
One half vote for Alfred E. Smith.

The galleries burst out with cheers and dancing. "You got guts!" shouted one spectator.

Elmer A. Carter, an alternate, rushed into the stadium clad in a bathrobe to cast his vote for Smith. Another delegate frankly admitted that he did not know how he was going to vote until Curry gave him a signal. Farley's quiet remark from the stand that his half-vote was for Roosevelt drew laughter and applause from the audience. The New York roll call consumed another weary hour.

At the end of the roll call, Missouri changed its vote twice—to give Roosevelt eleven, and then twelve votes. Boss Pendergast was doling out his reserve votes, hoping to start a landslide of switches that would sweep through the convention. It never came. While the tellers were tallying the official vote, Farley sat on the platform waiting for some delegation to make the break that would start the bandwagon rush, but nothing happened. Walsh finally announced the official vote at 7:15 A.M.: 666¼ for Roosevelt, 203¾ for Smith, 90¼ for Garner, and the rest scattered among the other six candidates. "In all the history of the Democratic Party, whenever a man received the huge vote that Governor Roosevelt did on that first ballot, he was nominated without delay," Farley wrote afterward, "but nothing happened. I was bitterly disappointed, and the realization that almost two years of heartbreaking work was about to go for nothing sent me into action at once."

The second ballot began immediately. The Connecticut delegation made a motion to adjourn, but since the balloting had begun, Walsh ruled the motion out of order. Farley raced around the convention floor, trying to find someone who could come up with the votes to put his candidate over. Cermak was sorry, but he could not make a move without a caucus and, with the balloting already in progress, it was too late. McAdoo could do nothing, he told Farley, until and unless John Garner released his delegates. Pendergast promised to release six more votes to Farley, to cover any loss of votes that might show on the Roosevelt score on the second ballot. Farley glumly returned to the rostrum to await the verdict and to hope again for a saving break in the ranks at the end of the tally. Again he hoped and waited in vain. The official count showed a gain of eleven votes for Roosevelt, bringing his total to 677¼.

The Oklahoma delegation, having shown its loyalty to Alfalfa Bill on the first ballot, began to desert him, and capriciously cast twenty-two votes for Will Rogers. By the third ballot, Governor Murray's name had disappeared from the reading clerk's tally sheet.

There was some discussion of the advisability of taking a third roll call. It was already 8 A.M., and the delegates were numb with weariness. Frank Hague insisted that a third ballot would show Roosevelt's strength beginning to crumble, and the beginning of a drift away from him. Farley was agreeable. He had some more reserve votes to throw into the breach and keep Roosevelt's vote climbing. The yawning clerk began to call the roll for the third time.

Another crisis occurred in the midst of the balloting. Mississippi's Pat Harrison, under the impression that there would be no further ballots, had returned to his hotel room and was preparing to go to bed when he turned on the radio and heard the convention clerk announce, "Mississippi passes." In a panic, he realized that a third ballot was being taken and that his delegation, evenly divided, nine and one-half votes for Baker, nine and one-half for Roosevelt, was unable to vote as a unit-rule delegation. Harrison hurtled back to the stadium, half dressed, in time to cast the deciding vote and keep Mississippi in the Roosevelt column.

Hague's prediction, like so many of his predictions, proved wrong. On the third ballot, the Roosevelt count inched up to 682. Garner gained ten votes, and Smith's total declined slightly, to 190¼. One incontrovertible fact could be read in the vote: the convention was deadlocked.

After the roll call, Arthur Mullen, the weary, disheveled Roosevelt floor leader, held a brief press conference. The fight was far from over, he said:

> We have taken a new poll of our rockbound strength, and it convinces us that 650 of our delegates will stay here until Roosevelt is nominated or until hell freezes over. If the emissaries of corrupt interests continue to halt the nomination of the man who is clearly the choice of the majority of the party, we shall speak out. We will denounce the damnable hypocrisy of the people who misrule New York City, Jersey City and Chicago, coming here to stand behind Mr. Smith in an effort to seize the power in the nation or else throw the party on the rocks.

Mullen, as a Nebraskan, echoed the sentiments of a large majority of the Western and Southern delegates in their absolute rejection of Al Smith, but as far as Roosevelt was concerned, their loyalty was not unshakable. As Mullen spoke, many of them were looking to other candidates who might be able to overcome the votes of the Smith bloc. Some, as witnessed by the third-ballot switch of Oklahoma votes to John Garner, had already found a new hero.

"We did little more than hold our own on that ballot," said Farley, later. "Our situation was desperate. There were indications that we could not hold our delegates through the fourth ballot."

Thousands of rumpled, bone-weary, stubble-chinned delegates, alternates and observers shuffled out of the stadium into the bright July morning, at 9 A.M., leaving behind them sixty tons of waste paper and debris, five thousand whiskey, gin, and pop bottles, $14,000 worth of camera equipment, twenty thousand used flashlight bulbs, and Mrs. J. Hamilton Lewis's pocketbook. It took 75,000 gallons of disinfectant to clean up the place. Surveying the scene from the press loft, H. L. Mencken wrote, "Most [of the delegates] are beyond middle life and many show obvious signs of oxidization. Two have died since the convention began, a matter of only five days." The convention was, he added, "the Democrats' quadrennial suicide pact."

Many of the rank and file delegates could look forward to the soothing restorative of a bath and a few hours sleep before the convention resumed its balloting in the evening. But there could be no rest for Jim Farley. He had to find 89 votes, and he had just ten hours to find them.

CHAPTER 13

THE SWITCH THAT MADE HISTORY

The aura of defeat hung like a thunderhead over Roosevelt head-quarters. The morning newspapers expressed the mood of the convention in a quotation from Paul McNutt: "The Roosevelt vote was disappointing. Otherwise, Indiana would have led the bandwagon parade." From Smith's headquarters came the flat announcement, "We have Roosevelt licked." There were signs of defection from a dozen delegations. The Roosevelt delegate support was disintegrating, and it seemed that only a miracle could prevent a complete collapse of his candidacy when the fourth ballot was cast.

On his way back from the stadium, Farley mentally narrowed the field where he might find the crucial votes to save the day for Roosevelt. Ritchie's hidden strength in the Southern and Midwestern delegations was defecting rapidly to Newton Baker, and he could no longer provide an answer. All that Farley could be certain of from Ritchie were the twenty-one votes of Maryland, and they were not enough to start a landslide. Farley had offered Ritchie the Vice-Presidential nomination on the night before the balloting began, moreover, and had been turned down. Byrd, with just twenty-six votes at his command, was not any more attractive. Howe's efforts to win the Virginians had come to nothing. Despite his promise in April that Roosevelt could have Virginia's votes when he needed them, Byrd now seemed more aloof than ever. Murray was never a consideration; indeed, the third ballot had disclosed the colorful governor's inability to control even his own delegation, when eleven Oklahoma votes switched to Reed and Garner.

The only thing that could possibly save the Roosevelt candidacy was a massive transfusion of delegate strength in the fourth ballot, and the only possible place to get it was the Texas-California coalition. Farley pinned all his last hopes on Sam Rayburn. As soon as he returned to the Congress, he summoned Frank Walker, Vincent Dailey of New York, Ed Flynn, and Pat Harrison to a strategy meeting.

They first went to tell Louis Howe of their last-ditch plans. The frail old man was in bad condition after a long night spent between the telephone and the radio. He was lying on the floor between two electric fans, his head propped up on a pillow, his shirt unbuttoned, with a radio nearby. Farley knelt on the floor and whispered his plans into Howe's ear. Howe nodded, but with no enthusiasm. He still had no hope that anything could be gained by negotiating with the supporters of Garner.

Senator Harrison telephoned Rayburn, who agreed to a meeting in the hotel suite Harrison shared with George Allen, a Mississippi-born commissioner of the District of Columbia and friend of several presidents. Farley went immediately to Harrison's apartment to wait for the Texans, and the others left to confer with the chiefs of rebellious delegations. While he was waiting for Rayburn, Farley fell asleep in a chair. At Allen's suggestion, he moved to a bed and was sleeping soundly when Rayburn and Silliman Evans arrived.

The meeting was brief, almost curt. Farley did not need to tell the taciturn Texan how desperate the Roosevelt cause had become. As usual, Rayburn made no promises. He simply said, "We'll see what can be done." Farley's hopes soared again, and he went to tell Howe about the meeting. Howe was still unimpressed. "That's fine," he said dully.

Another effort was being made at that moment to persuade Garner to release his delegates to Roosevelt, but Jim Farley had no knowledge of it. On the previous evening, while the first ballot was being taken, Joe Kennedy made a long distance call to the Hearst ranch at San Simeon. John Neylan, a San Francisco lawyer who was Hearst's chief legal counsel, received the call and repeated what Kennedy said to Hearst, who was standing next to him. Kennedy said bluntly that Roosevelt did not have enough votes to win the nomination, and that Ritchie had been displaced by Baker as the convention's alternate candidate. Baker, he said, had more than one hundred second-choice votes pledged to him. "Kennedy was an operator," says Arthur Krock, who was in the room with him when he made the telephone call. "Hearst didn't make a move until Kennedy said that he was going to get Newton D. Baker as the nominee unless he spoke to Garner. Garner would listen to him, he said, since he owed the California delegation entirely to Hearst. When Kennedy quit talking to Neylan, Hearst made his move."

On the floor of the convention, in the meanwhile, Dan Roper had offered McAdoo the office of Secretary of State in a Roosevelt administration, as the price of swinging California's vote. Roper made the offer with no authority to do so, but McAdoo turned it down and asked instead to be consulted and to have veto power over all of Roosevelt's choices for his cabinet. If Roosevelt agreed, said McAdoo, "if I can get a recess of the convention so I can take a poll of the California delegation, I'll endeavor to get them behind Roosevelt, and that will mean Texas, too." He warned Roper, though, that Hearst's representatives within the delegation were insisting that California cast at least seven ballots for Garner before backing another candidate. That would be too late, Roper told him: Roosevelt could not survive seven ballots, and the convention would inevitably turn either to Baker or to Smith. "I am told that there are over one hundred ballots already pledged to Baker as second choice," he added.

Roper returned to the Congress Hotel while the balloting was going on, to tell Howe about his conversation with McAdoo. They immediately called Albany and told Roosevelt what McAdoo's terms were. Roosevelt agreed to give McAdoo a voice in his cabinet making. No one seemed to realize that only John Garner could release the California delegation.

Just before the tense first ballot, Arthur Mullen spoke to Tom Connally in yet another effort to wean away the Texas delegates. "If Garner will take the vice presidency," he assured Connally, "an arrangement can be made to have him get it." Neither man was aware of Farley's previous offers to Sam Rayburn. "Let's adjourn," said Connally, "and see what we can do." But Connally's motions for adjournment failed, and any action either by Connally or McAdoo was indefinitely postponed.

In California, however, Hearst was acting quickly. After a lengthy call to Colonel Willicombe in Chicago, which confirmed his deepest fears of a sudden switch to Newton Baker, Hearst sent a telegram to George Rothwell Brown, one of his correspondents in Washington:

MR. HEARST IS FEARFUL THAT WHEN ROOSEVELT STRENGTH CRUMBLES IT WILL BRING ABOUT EITHER THE ELECTION OF SMITH OR

BAKER. EITHER WOULD BE DISASTROUS. TELL GARNER THAT THE
CHIEF BELIEVES NOTHING CAN NOW SAVE THE COUNTRY BUT FOR
HIM TO THROW HIS VOTES TO GOVERNOR ROOSEVELT.

Brown was a confidant of Garner's, and had written a flattering
campaign biography, *The Speaker of the House.* He had no difficulty arranging an appointment. Garner received him in the Speaker's Room at the
Capitol at 11 A.M. on the morning after the convention's marathon session.
After Garner had read Hearst's message, he said, "Say to Mr. Hearst that I
fully agree with him. He is right. Tell him I will carry out his suggestion
and release my delegates to Roosevelt."

At 3 P.M., Garner called Rayburn at his headquarters in Chicago.
He was terse, as always. "Sam," he said, "I think it is time to break this thing
up. Roosevelt is the choice of the convention. Hell, I'll do anything to see
the Democrats win one more national election." Rayburn was unhappy with
Garner's decision, but he knew better than to argue with him. He knew, too,
that the Texas delegation was in no mood to desert their hero. All he could
do was to get Garner to promise to think it over and call him again in three
hours and reconfirm his decision.

There were several other versions of how the switch was made.
Mullen, Roper, McAdoo, and scores of others boasted, or felt, that they
were responsible. Rayburn and other partisans of Garner insisted that the
decision to switch had been made by the Speaker alone. Perhaps Garner
had already made up his mind before he saw the message from Hearst, but
there can be no doubt that he followed Hearst's advice. Basil O'Connor told
Roosevelt that, "of the 55,000 Democrats said to be in Chicago, 62,000 are
going to claim credit for the switch."

Howe and Farley were not told that the tide had turned, and the
gloom that pervaded the Roosevelt headquarters grew with each hour and
each new bit of information. The Mississippi delegation had switched its
allegiance to Baker after two heated caucuses. Arkansas was reported crum-
bling—which might signal a general retreat from Roosevelt, for Arkansas
was fourth in the roll of states and territories. The leaders of Tammany Hall
were seeking a new, compromise candidate to be offered to the convention
when Roosevelt went down to defeat.

A rumor that Alabama would defect to another candidate, presum-
ably Baker, was stifled by ex-Governor William W. Brandon, of "24 votes
for Underwood" fame. The nation's Democrats "will not submit to the
dictation of a few cities like Jersey City, Tammany New York and Boston,"
he vowed. Alabama would continue to vote for Roosevelt until he was

elected. But news of a rising anti-Roosevelt trend came from the delegations of Iowa, Minnesota, and Michigan. Test balloting indicated that Illinois and Indiana were realigning for Al Smith. Conferences and caucuses went on endlessly. At Roosevelt headquarters, the conviction grew that only California and Texas could save the day. "They looked to these as the sisters of Bluebeard's wife looked to the highway for the help which alone could avert tragedy," reported Arthur Krock.

In Albany, the mood was not so gloomy, although the Governor was clearly disappointed. His mother, old Sara Roosevelt, had gone home to Hyde Park after listening to the first ballot, but the rest of the family and their friends had sat up through the night around the radio in the study. Another radio had been set up in the ballroom, where the members of the press were gathered, and a third in a back room where the state troopers assigned to guard the Governor were stationed. After the convention adjourned, Roosevelt talked to Howe on the telephone and, on Howe's suggestion, sent a telegram to Chicago:

I AM IN THIS FIGHT TO STAY. PLEASE THANK ALL THE DELEGATES VOTING FOR ME.

THIS IS A BATTLE FOR PRINCIPLE. A CLEAR MAJORITY OF THE CONVENTION UNDERSTANDS THAT IT IS BEING WAGED TO KEEP OUR PARTY AS A WHOLE FROM DICTATION BY A SMALL GROUP REPRESENTING THE INTERESTS IN THE NATION WHICH HAVE NO PLACE IN OUR PARTY.

MY FRIENDS WILL NOT BE MISLED BY ORGANIZED PROPAGANDA BY TELEGRAMS NOW BEING SENT TO DELEGATES.

STICK TO YOUR GUNS. IT IS CLEAR THAT THE NATION MUST NOT AND SHALL NOT BE OVERRIDDEN. NOW IS THE TIME TO MAKE IT CLEAR THAT WE INTEND TO STAND FAST AND WIN.

At 6 P.M. Chicago time, the lobbies of the Hotel Sherman resembled Macy's on Christmas Eve. Hundreds of delegates gathered in noisy huddles everywhere, and rumors eddied through the chattering groups like the smoke from their cigars and cigarettes. The California and Texas delegations had scheduled caucuses in adjoining rooms at the Sherman. When Sam Rayburn called the Texans together, only a few more than the majority necessary to form a quorum were present. More than seventy Texas delegates, elated over Garner's gains in the bloody third ballot, were scattered all over the city, in hotels, restaurants, and speakeasies, recruiting more votes for the Speaker.

The caucus had just rejected the pleas of seventeen delegates with four and a quarter votes to cast to let them vote for Roosevelt when a message was brought to Rayburn that the Speaker was on the telephone. Rayburn asked the delegates to wait for him, explaining that he "might have some important news." In the corridor, on his way to the telephone, he encountered McAdoo, who was on his way to the California caucus. "Sam, we'll vote for Jack Garner until hell freezes over, if you say so," McAdoo said, apparently forgetting his promise to Dan Roper. Rayburn told him that he was on his way to talk to Garner and get his official release. He advised McAdoo to go to his caucus and release the votes to Roosevelt.

Rayburn's conversation with Garner was brief indeed. Garner said nothing more than "yes," twice, when Mister Sam asked him if he still wanted to release his delegates to Roosevelt and if this could be considered an official release.

When he returned to the caucus, Rayburn was glum. "Well, John is out," he told the delegates. "He asks me to thank all of you from the bottom of his heart for your loyalty and to tell you that the instructions binding you are no longer in force. He releases you without any strings whatsoever."

The stunned delegates reacted to the announcement with an angry roar. "We don't care what John wants," shouted a big Texas ranger. "We are with him and we are going to stick!" A large group, led by Amon Carter, urged the delegation to stand fast for John Garner. The caucus was in an uproar. Women wept. Two Illinois delegates slipped into the room and promised that Garner would pick up thirty votes from their delegation if he continued as a candidate.

Rayburn was able to bring the meeting to order at last, and, after hearing many sad and angry speeches, the delegation voted, by the hairline margin of 54 to 51, to support Roosevelt. "We did the best we could for John," said Silliman Evans. "We wish he'd won."

No one will ever know how the vote might have gone if the seventy-odd absentees had been present. It is reasonable to assume, though, that since most of them were Garner diehards, out recruiting votes, they would have stuck to their candidate, whether he wanted them to or not, and the history of the 1932 convention might have been quite different.

In the next room, the California caucus was almost as stormy. It had been summoned on the insistence of two delegates, Thomas N. Storke, a newspaper publisher from Santa Barbara, and Hamilton Cotton, a Los Angeles oil millionaire. The two were known to be close to McAdoo. Two San Francisco financiers, both Republicans, cornered Cotton in an elevator on his way back from the all-night session and asked him to try to swing the delegation to Newton Baker. They were prepared to finance Baker's and McAdoo's California campaigns, they said, if Baker got the nod. All day long, Storke and Cotton were harassed by a parade of Roosevelt supporters, who came to their room, or kept the telephone ringing insistently, to argue and plead for a switch by California to the man in Albany. A flood of telegrams from pro-Roosevelt Californians arrived. Josephus Daniels, Dan Roper, Mrs. Daisy Borden Harriman—a *doyenne* of Washington society and a lifelong friend of the Roosevelt family—and Mrs. Isabella Greenway all turned up to apply the pressure personally. Finally, the persistent Mrs. Greenway persuaded the two to call on Farley. At the meeting Storke told Farley that, while he thought California would go to Roosevelt eventually, he felt the delegation would stick with Garner for another ballot or two.

That would be too late, Farley told them flatly. "Baker will be nominated." He had thrown every available vote into the third ballot, he said, keeping nothing in reserve. Unless California switched on the next ballot, the Roosevelt candidacy was doomed. With eyes brimming, Farley told them, "Five states that have been held in the Roosevelt column by the unit issue—Minnesota, Iowa, the two Dakotas, and Mississippi—will break and scatter on the fourth ballot." After that, it would be too late to retrieve the situation for Roosevelt.

Storke and Cotton were finally convinced and rushed off to McAdoo's hotel suite. After some hesitation, he agreed to call the caucus. When the delegates had assembled and McAdoo had told them of Garner's release and Roosevelt's critical situation, the delegates broke into an excited roar. Several declared for Baker, but more were loyal to Garner. "We came here to vote for John Nance Garner and no one else!" screamed Grace Bryan Hargreaves. "McAdoo, you are attempting to betray us!" shouted another delegate.

Possibly a majority of the Californians supported Roosevelt as a second choice, but a bloc of San Francisco delegates held out for Al Smith. It was clear that the delegation was badly split. If California cast a ballot divided among four or five candidates, other delegations would be encouraged to scatter their own votes in the same way, and Roosevelt might be lost in a fragmented convention.

After much argument, John Elliott, another oil man and a skilled political manipulator, suggested a compromise solution: instead of polling the delegation, why not select a committee of three delegates, under the supervision of McAdoo, "to determine when, and to whom, the vote of California should go"? The delegation gave its unenthusiastic approval to Elliott's resolution and elected a panel of three. Before leaving for the convention, the committee met secretly and agreed to pledge California's 44 votes to Roosevelt on the fourth ballot. It was also agreed that the decision would be kept in strict secrecy until McAdoo announced California's choice. As a result, all but four of the delegates had no idea how their votes would be cast, or on what ballot, and Roosevelt picked up 44 votes without the formality of a poll of the California delegation.

At Roosevelt headquarters, in the meanwhile, Silliman Evans brought the good news from Texas. Howe promptly relayed it to Albany. Farley got on the telephone to inform the Mississippians and the other stray delegations. They promptly returned to the Roosevelt fold. The bandwagon, after being stalled so long and coming so close to a wreck, was rolling again.

It had been a bad afternoon for Farley. A report that John Curry had been seen talking earnestly to Sam Rayburn was brought to him. Farley was worried for fear that Garner might be persuaded to stay in the fight. Curry and Garner were friendly, he knew, and the Tammany bloc of Representatives in Congress had always been especially cooperative with the little Speaker. An offer of New York's Tammany votes might encourage Garner and undo all of Farley's plans and hopes.

Al Smith heard about Curry's conversation with Rayburn and he resented the possibility that the Tammany leader might be bartering votes that were pledged to him to keep Garner in the race. While it was true that Garner was all-important to the anti-Roosevelt confederacy, Smith still, at that late hour, cherished the notion that he could emerge from the carnage of a Roosevelt defeat as the ultimate choice of the convention. That afternoon five hundred telegrams, all urging support of Al Smith, were delivered to the New York delegation.

After the caucus, McAdoo telephoned Hearst in California with an alternate plan of action. Why not switch Texas and California's votes again —there was still time—behind someone other than Roosevelt? Why not William Gibbs McAdoo? He would be a much better candidate than Roosevelt, McAdoo assured the publisher. Hearst turned him down flatly. He did not want to run the risk of letting Smith or Baker run off with the nomination, and Roosevelt was the only candidate with sufficient votes to offer a focal point for the ninety Texas-California votes. Roosevelt was the only candidate Hearst could be sure of, and the decision should stand. Later, McAdoo suggested himself as a good choice for the Vice-Presidential nomination, and again Hearst turned him down. The choice, he said, belonged to the Presidential candidate.

When Howe called Albany with the glad tidings, the tense mood that permeated the Executive Mansion gave way to a feeling of excitement and expectation. "We're ready for action," Roosevelt said, when the time came to turn on the radio and tune in on the convention. He looked relaxed and extremely fit, after his sleepless night. He was wearing a white suit and flourishing his cigarette holder, settled in a large armchair with his little black scottie, Megs, at his feet. His sons John and Elliott were nearby, drawing up tally sheets. His mother was sitting next to him, knitting, and Eleanor Roosevelt, also knitting, was in a far corner of the room. Also with the Governor were his sister-in-law, Mrs. James Roosevelt, and Sam and Dorothy Rosenman. Grace Tully and Missy Lehand tuned the radio.

Rumors that McAdoo was switching California's votes reached Al Smith in his hotel suite before the caucuses were over and the votes had been tallied. He telephoned Baruch at once. "Bernie," he said, "your long-legged friend has run out on us, just as I thought he would." Baruch was astonished. "Why, Al, you must be mistaken," he said. "No, I ain't mistaken," Smith told him. "You'll find out." A few minutes later, Baruch called back with confirmation: "Well, Al, I guess you're right. He's in caucus now and wouldn't come out and see the man I sent down."

Smith made one last effort to stem the tide. He asked Belle Moskowitz, his personal secretary and political advisor, to try to get Garner on the telephone. When she could not get through, Smith took the telephone and personally placed a call to the Washington Hotel, where the Speaker made his home. He managed to talk to Mrs. Garner, in her apartment. Smith explained who he was and asked to talk to the Speaker. Mrs. Garner told him that he had just gone out and asked Smith to call back again in twenty minutes. When he returned the call, Smith was answered by a hotel clerk. "Yes, Governor," said the clerk, "I'll get the Speaker for you. I know just where he is."

For ten minutes, Al Smith fretted on the telephone, until the clerk returned and told him that he could not find Speaker Garner. That was too bad, said Smith; it was an urgent matter. "Governor," the clerk blurted out, "I'm a friend of yours, and I'm going to tell you the truth. He's up on the roof eating dinner, but he don't want to talk to you." Al Smith had reached the end of the political road.

Later that evening, John Garner lingered on the hotel roof garden, pacing nervously up and down, glancing down now and then at the illuminated White House. *Time* magazine reported the scene:

> As he walked up and down alone, his cigar made a nasturtium-colored spot in the darkness.
> "Mr. Speaker," asked a voice at his elbow, "you've gone to Roosevelt?"

"That's right, son." The Speaker recognized a newshawk from *The New York Times.* "I'm a little older than you are, son, and politics is funny."

Beyond the black outline of the Treasury, the White House gleamed in the night. Speaker Garner lighted a fresh cigar. It was too dark to see the expression in his eyes.

When Smith called to tell him of the switch, Frank Hague rushed off to see Rayburn with an offer to swing New Jersey's delegates behind Garner if he would reverse his decision. Rayburn shook his head. It was too late, he said. The Speaker had made up his mind.

One delegate who had not heard of the switch was Daniel F. Cohalan of Tammany Hall. He stopped by the table, in the Congress dining room, where Tom Walsh was having dinner with Delegate Ambrose O'Connell of Iowa. "We have Roosevelt stopped, Senator," Cohalan announced pleasantly, "and I'd like to have authority to present your name to the convention as a compromise candidate." Walsh coolly refused.

In an effort to get Tammany's delegates on the bandwagon, Farley called on John Curry and John McGooey in their hotel suite. Jimmie Walker was with them when Farley walked in with his news. "They couldn't believe me," Farley reported. "They told me that Hague had said Roosevelt was stopped. I assured them that there had been a switch. They asked me where, and I told them to come to the convention. Walker was so shocked he led me into the bedroom and made me repeat myself."

Farley was too excited and nervous to eat his dinner. He left the hotel dining room before the main course was served and hurried to the taxi stand. The Chicago Stadium was electric with excitement. Word of the Texas-California shift had reached most of the delegations, but the spectators in the galleries were unaware of what had happened. They expected to see Roosevelt go down in defeat and when, after the first few minutes of the roll call, McAdoo asked permission to speak from the platform, they had no idea what was about to happen.

For William McAdoo, standing before the hushed convention, it must have been a moment of exquisite triumph. A tall, lanky man with gray hair, an enormous collar that looked as if it should choke him, and heavy-lidded eyes that had an habitual look of skepticism in them, he stood quietly aside while Tom Walsh gaveled down a few scattered boos from the galleries. Watching McAdoo, H. L. Mencken wrote, "Eight years ago in New York he led the hosts of the Invisible Empire against the Pope, the rum demon and all the other Beelzebubs of the Hookworm Belt and came so close to getting the nomination that the memory of its loss must still shiver him." The man who blocked him was Al Smith, and now he was paying Al back.

"If revenge is really sweet, he was sucking a sugar teat."

Farley did not know it at the time, but McAdoo very nearly missed his moment of revenge, and Roosevelt could conceivably have missed his moment of triumph. A mile from the Sherman Hotel on his way to the convention hall, McAdoo was dismayed when his limousine stopped suddenly and his chauffeur announced that they were out of gas.* McAdoo made the rest of the trip on the back of a policeman's motorcycle, in a taxi cab, and on foot. When he made his breathless entrance into the hall, Arkansas' chairman was just announcing the delegation's vote (eighteen for Roosevelt). California was next on the roster of the states. If McAdoo had been delayed another minute or two, California would have had to pass, since the Chairman alone had the authority to announce the vote.

In that event, almost anything might have happened. The next dramatic shift would be Texas, and Texas was far down the roll call of the states. In between were the maverick states—Iowa, Minnesota, Mississippi, and the Dakotas—and while they had been lured back to the Roosevelt corral by Farley, there was no reason why they could not caucus again, in the absence of a California vote, and start a stampede to Baker and other candidates. At that point, Roosevelt's majority was strung together on such a fragile thread that almost any unscheduled event could send it flying in every direction.

McAdoo may have owed his timely arrival to the unruly friends of Al Smith in the galleries, who greeted the announcement of Arizona's choice (six votes for Roosevelt) with prolonged boos and catcalls. It took Chairman Walsh several minutes to restore order. It would have been a supreme irony if Al Smith's cheering section had shown better behavior at that moment and Roosevelt had gone down to defeat because of their polite silence.

The hall was certainly quiet and expectant as McAdoo began to speak:

---

* Limousines for the delegation chairmen were furnished by the Chicago Committee on Arrangements and Entertainment, and Mayor Cermak and his fellow politicians in Chicago were Smith partisans. When McAdoo was told that his chauffeur was known to be quite friendly with some Smith enthusiasts, he decided—and believed to his dying day—that the gasoline had been deliberately drained from the car in order to prevent him from getting to the convention on time.

Mr. Chairman, ladies and gentlemen, I thank you for the privilege accorded me to say just a word in explaining the vote of the State of California. California came here to nominate a President of the United States. She did not come here to deadlock this convention, or to engage in another desolating contest like that of 1924.

In my great state, where Democracy has increased its registration this year 143 percent, we believe that the interests of the people of the United States will be best conserved by a change from a Republican administration to a Democratic administration. We think that a useless contest on this floor, long prolonged, would only lead to schisms in the party that could not be cured, perhaps, before the election.

Sometimes in major operations, when skilled surgery is required, the life of the patient may be destroyed if there is unnecessary delay. We believe, therefore, that California should take a stand here tonight that will bring this contest to a swift, and, we hope, satisfactory conclusion—a stand taken with the utmost unselfishness and regardless of our own views of the situation—a stand prompted by the fact that when any man comes into this convention with the popular will behind him to the extent of almost seven hundred votes——

At that moment, a cheer from the Roosevelt delegations began, rose in volume and spread across the floor, except in the silent sections occupied by the delegations of New York, New Jersey, and New England. A spontaneous demonstration took over the darkened hall, and the huge spotlights picked out the figures of dancing, flag-waving delegates. The Texans let out a piercing rebel yell, and one delegate ran down the aisle to present the Lone Star flag to McAdoo.

When the demonstration had almost died out, the audience in the galleries, just beginning to sense what was happening, unloosed a furious outburst of boos, curses and shrieks. Between the cheers from the floor and the thunder from above, the convention was a scene from a madhouse. Walsh, flushed and tight-lipped, beat his gavel in vain, and finally called on Cermak to restore order. The booing turned to cheers when the Mayor reached the microphone. "Let me appeal to my friends in the galleries," he shouted. "Please act like guests. I appeal to you, allow this gathering to go back home with nothing but pleasant memories of our city." Cermak's entreaties were wasted, and the crowd continued to scream its disapproval.

McAdoo resumed his speech, bending down to shout into the microphone, against the angry obbligato of the galleries:

Judge for the future whether or not this is the kind of hospitality Chicago accords its guests [he screamed]. I intend to say what I propose to say here tonight regardless of what the galleries or anyone else thinks.

As I was saying when this demonstration began, my friends, whenever a man comes into this convention with seven hundred votes in his favor, I take it as indicative of the public sentiment, and I believe in democracy and the rule of the majority, and the two-thirds majority, which makes it very difficult in Democratic conventions to nominate any man. I say that when any man is within reach of the two thirds that are necessary to nominate him, he is entitled to the nomination. And California proposes to do her share to see that the popular will is respected.

We came here for the great Texan, John N. Garner. We have lost not one whit of the love and respect in which we hold that great statesman. He is worthy of the highest place that you could give him, but he hasn't as many votes as Mr. Roosevelt, and I want to say that Mr. Garner himself is in accord with the position I take here tonight.

The great State of Texas and the great State of California are acting in accordance with what we believe to be the best, first for America, and next for the Democratic Party, and I want to create no wounds. I had a very ineffectual part in the wounds that were created against my wish in 1924.

I would like to see Democrats fight Republicans, and not Democrats, and if this party is worthy of the respect and confidence of the American people, it will conduct itself in such a way that when its decision is finally announced about these candidates, we can go forth to the American people with confidence that our decision represents the will of these delegates, even though all of them may not believe that the course we take is right.

I have never seen a Democratic convention which agreed unanimously, except where everybody else except the successful man had been licked, and that was the man who ought to be named President of the United States.

With that, McAdoo raised his hands over his head and bellowed into the microphone, "And so, my friends, California casts forty-four votes for Franklin Delano Roosevelt!"

Bedlam broke out again, a cacophonous din of cheers and boos, accompanied by the band and the organ. While McAdoo was speaking, the leaders of dissident delegations began to appear at the back of the rostrum, and by the time he had finished, a crowd of delegates and state standards had gathered behind him, waiting to climb aboard the bandwagon. Farley pushed through the crowd to pound McAdoo on the back. Anton Cermak seized the microphone to announce the release of Illinois' 58 votes. Paul McNutt offered up Indiana's thirty. Franklin Roosevelt, Jr., stood beside Farley on the rostrum, surveying the tumult on the floor. His brother, Jimmy, smilingly received congratulations in the middle of a swarm of delegates.

The roll of the states continued, and one by one they fell in line, except for New York and the four other Eastern states committed to Smith. There was no message from Smith releasing his delegates and in the final tally 201½ irreconcilable votes were cast for him. In the rush to get on the bandwagon, several *presidenciables* appeared, in the new role of *vice presidenciable*. Albert Ritchie personally announced Maryland's switch, and James Reed took the stand to thank his supporters. "At this hour," he intoned, "I summon Democracy to rally to the standard." John Curry announced the release of the New York delegation. "The convention has decided," he said. "We are all good Democrats." The good Democrats of the Tammany delegation had decided otherwise though, and, with no word from Al Smith, they stayed with their candidate to the end.

At 10:32 P.M., with 942 ballots cast for Roosevelt, Chairman Walsh solemnly announced, "I proclaim him the nominee of this convention for President of the United States."

Roosevelt, in his Albany study, grinned happily when he heard the climactic moment of McAdoo's speech on the radio. "Good old McAdoo," he said. Eleanor Roosevelt and the two secretaries embraced, and young John and Elliott threw their tally sheets in the air. Farley called from his tiny office in the stadium to offer his congratulations. Howe and the staff at Roosevelt headquarters celebrated with champagne in paper cups.

A crowd gathered in front of the Executive Mansion, and Roosevelt, aided by his son Elliott, went to a window to greet them. "My chief regret," he told them, "is that I will not be governor again, and continue to be among you as a neighbor." Eleanor Roosevelt went to the kitchen and put an apron over her green chiffon dress to scramble some eggs. "And bring those frankfurters from the icebox," she told the butler. "The boys will like them." A reporter who interviewed her as she prepared the eggs asked her about her own plans. "It will be like everything else in the world," she said. "I'll have to wait until I find out what I can do." The governor, she said, was "prepared for anything tonight. I think he took it very calmly.

But I have never seen him very excited. He was always calm, whether in victory or defeat."

Within a few minutes of McAdoo's announcement, Roosevelt sent a telegram which Walsh read at the end of the balloting:

IT IS WITH A DEEP SENSE OF MY RESPONSIBILITY TO MEET YOUR HIGH ESTIMATE OF MY QUALIFICATIONS THAT I THANK YOU FOR MY SELECTION AS YOUR CANDIDATE.

IT IS CUSTOMARY TO HOLD FORMAL NOTIFICATION CERE-MONIES SOME WEEKS AFTER THE CONVENTION. THIS INVOLVES GREAT EXPENSE, AND IN THESE TIMES I WOULD PREFER THAT THIS BE NOT FOLLOWED. INSTEAD, MAY I ASK THE CONVENTION TO REMAIN IN SESSION AFTER THE SELECTION OF THE VICE PRESI-DENTIAL CANDIDATE TOMORROW, THAT I MAY APPEAR BEFORE YOU AND BE NOTIFIED AT THAT TIME?

I WANT VERY MUCH TO EXPRESS MY THANKS TO YOU ALL PERSONALLY AND FACE TO FACE.

WILL YOU LET ME KNOW THE WISHES OF THE CONVENTION? I CAN ARRIVE BETWEEN 2 AND 3 O'CLOCK TOMORROW.

The message was received with wild applause. Even the people in the galleries applauded. The flight to Chicago was a dramatic gesture and, in 1932, a daring one. *The New York Times* boasted to its readers that late editions had been sent to the delegates in Chicago each day by chartered plane, in just seven and a half hours. Franklin Roosevelt's distant cousin, Theodore Roosevelt, was the only previous president or nominee to fly, and that was a very brief trip, a fifteen-minute flight over Washington.

Tom Walsh sent a jubilant wire to Albany:

THE CONVENTION EXTENDS ITS GREETINGS AND ASSURANCES OF FEALTY TO ITS NOMINEE, AND WELCOMES THE NEWS THAT HE WILL BE HERE WITH US TOMORROW.

In Washington, Speaker Garner was asleep when the nominating ballots were cast. He was awakened at 11 P.M. with the news that Roose-velt had won and got up long enough to send his own good wishes to Albany: HEARTIEST CONGRATULATIONS. YOUR NOMINATION MEANS YOUR ELECTION.

Al Smith listened to the opening of the balloting at his headquarters for a few minutes, then barked, "Haul that radio in here," and retired to a back room, where he listened in bitter silence, chewing on an unlit cigar. Only once, when Connecticut loyally voted for him and the galleries cheered, did the flicker of a smile cross his face. Staff assistants were packing up Smith's posters, buttons, and campaign literature before McAdoo had finished speaking. When a reporter asked him if he intended to support the nominee, Smith snapped, "I have no comment to make." That night, Smith irreconcilables defaced Roosevelt posters in the hotel lobbies and tore them from the walls.

At a large midnight press conference James Farley solemnly insisted that "there were no deals, no promises, about places or other patronage offered leaders by us. The withdrawal by Speaker Garner from the contest was purely voluntary and was prompted as Mr. McAdoo said by a desire on Mr. Garner's part to prevent a deadlock and the will of the majority being registered by the convention." This was only partly true. Garner had, in fact, reached his decision on his own initiative—and an urgent suggestion from William Randolph Hearst. He had been offered the Vice Presidency at Farley's first meeting with Sam Rayburn, though, and Rayburn had spurned it. The second place had been dangled before Byrd, Ritchie, and perhaps others by Howe and Farley. The promise of being consulted in the selection of Roosevelt's cabinet had been made to McAdoo, and it was honored when Roosevelt began to consider names.[*] Years later, Farley agreed that the Vice Presidency had indeed been used as barter at the convention—but he made a fine distinction: "It wasn't offered to Garner. It was offered to me, to do what I could with it."

The press had some last words to say about Smith's failure. "Today another Roosevelt has the delegates and the galleries cannot move them," wrote William Allen White:

> Smith, a sturdier man and wiser than Bryan, saw the galleries thrill at his name, and knew that all the cheers, all the crashing of bands and the throbbing of drums were only hail and farewell to a leader beloved, but beaten and ignored.
>
> Somehow it was Smith's own fault. In this convention he has been saying catty things about Roosevelt—merely catty—not in Smith's best style.

In his epitaph for the unhappy warrior, Henry Mencken wrote,

> The failure of the opposition was the failure of Al Smith. From the moment he arrived on the ground it was apparent that he had no plan, and was animated only by his fierce hatred of Roosevelt, the

_____

[*] *One McAdoo-approved appointment was that of his friend, Dan Roper, to be Secretary of Commerce.*

cuckoo who had seized his nest. That hatred may have had logic in it, but it was important to organize the allies . . . Perhaps the Al of eight or ten years ago, or even of four years ago, might have achieved the miracle that the crisis called for, but it was far beyond the technique of the golf-playing Al of today.

Arthur Krock, who had been privy to the behind-the-scenes maneuvers of Joseph Kennedy and William Randolph Hearst, was surprised that Smith ever thought his coalition would work. "It is inexplicable," he wrote, "how Mr. Smith ever believed that Mr. McAdoo and Mr. Hearst would make common cause with him merely to accomplish one of Mr. Smith's personal desires. So long as their involved state seemed greater to them than to Mr. Smith's, they went along. But as soon as they perceived that only the Smith interest was being served, they broke the very fragile connection."

CHAPTER 14

"A NEW DEAL FOR THE AMERICAN PEOPLE"

Presidential nominees are usually accorded the privilege of selecting their running mates,* and in 1932 the convention awaited Franklin Roosevelt's choice. Farley suggested, in a telephone call to Albany, that John Garner should be given first refusal. Roosevelt agreed, although he knew that a Westerner would make a better-balanced ticket. Garner represented a region that would vote for the Democratic ticket—despite the retreat from Al Smith in 1928, the "solid South" was still Democratic territory. Sam Rayburn called Washington and made the offer, and Garner accepted. It was the first time Rayburn had mentioned the Vice Presidency to Garner. In view of his pungent belittling of the office just a few days earlier, his

---

* Not always, though. Harding had no voice in the selection of Calvin Coolidge in 1920. Dwight Eisenhower relegated the decision to a group of his closest advisers, who selected Richard Nixon in 1952. Adlai Stevenson left the choice to the convention in 1956, which precipitated a rough floor fight between Senators John F. Kennedy and Estes Kefauver. Kefauver won by a slim margin. In 1968, Richard Nixon picked Spiro Agnew on the advice and with the consent of Senator Strom Thurmond of South Carolina, who had been helpful in getting the support of Southern delegates for Nixon's nomination.

acceptance was surprising, but Rayburn explained that Garner was getting on—he was sixty-two years old—and would welcome a job that would be less demanding than the Speakership.

There were many other eager aspirants for the job. Bernard Baruch was one of the first to turn up at Roosevelt headquarters, hat in hand, to ask if it was too late to get Albert Ritchie on the ticket. Farley assured him that it was. McAdoo still thought that he was entitled to the job, but Howe told him to forget it—his nomination would remove any hope of getting the embittered forces of Al Smith to endorse the ticket. Burton Wheeler, Clarence Dill, and several other Westerners were very available candidates. Mayor Hague announced that he would place the name of Representative Mary T. Norton, the first woman Democrat to sit in Congress, before the convention, but withdrew when Garner's selection was made known. When the balloting began, early in the afternoon of July 2, Garner's only challenger was General Matthew A. Tinsley of Iowa, a war hero who had commanded the famous Rainbow Division in France.

Before leaving Albany, Roosevelt and Judge Rosenman put the finishing touches on his acceptance speech, which Rosenman had prepared during the crucial balloting with the help of a memorandum from Raymond Moley. The speech was to become a large bone of contention in Chicago. On the night of the nomination, Louis Howe called Albany and demanded that the final text of the speech be read to him over the telephone and transcribed by his secretary. Jealous of Rosenman's role in what he felt should be his own act, Howe summarily rejected the speech and began to write his own version. Fatigued and sick as he was, he spent the entire night writing.

Roosevelt and his party—his wife and two sons, three secretaries, two bodyguards and Sam Rosenman, who was terrified at the idea of air travel—left Albany Airport at 8:30 A.M. The candidate was in an ebullient mood. "It's a perfect day, isn't it?" he said to the reporters who had come to see him off. It was far from a perfect day for flying, however. The chartered plane, a trimotored, thirteen-passenger Ford craft, encountered strong headwinds that delayed the arrival in Chicago by more than two hours. The cabin was noisy and cold. Fourteen-year-old John Roosevelt became sick as soon as the plane was airborne and retreated to the tail section. A seat had been removed, to give the governor and Rosenman legroom. The two spent most of the flight revising the speech—the Rosenman version.

No members of the press were aboard the plane, though James Kieran, trying for a scoop for *The New York Times,* attempted to follow the Roosevelt plane in a chartered, single-engine monoplane but was grounded in Cleveland with engine trouble.

The Roosevelt plane landed twice for refueling, in Buffalo and Cleveland, and although Roosevelt never left his seat, he was greeted by enthusiastic crowds in both cities. In Cleveland, municipal officials asked Newton D. Baker to come with them to the airport, to greet the triumphant nominee. "I'm afraid I won't be able to do that," said Baker. "I'm very, very much occupied this morning."

Roosevelt was anxious to restore unity in the party as quickly as possible. When a reporter asked him, before he left Albany, if he expected to see Al Smith soon, he answered, "I certainly hope so." But Smith was determined to avoid a confrontation, and when he learned of the dramatic flight, he decided to get out of Chicago as quickly as possible. A notice appeared in the lobby of the Congress Hotel: "The true friends of Governor Smith will accompany him back to New York on the afternoon train." Smith stayed in seclusion in his suite, brooding over his defeat. Raskob and Shouse called on him, and had a long, solemn conference. At breakfast, he read some of the two hundred telegrams he had received, urging him to form a third party. Before he checked out of the hotel he saw Frank Hague briefly.

In order to avert any possibility of an encounter with Roosevelt, Smith and his party left the Congress more than an hour before they could board their train, and rode around the city to while away the time. They slipped out of a side entrance of the hotel in order to avoid the large crowds of people who were already gathering in front of the Michigan Avenue entrance to welcome Roosevelt. Hundreds of loyal supporters accompanied Smith on his trip home.

Roosevelt learned of Smith's seething reaction to his nomination just before he left for Chicago. He asked Dorothy Rosenman to see if she could get someone to intercept Smith before he arrived in New York and persuade him not to say anything to the press that might split the party irretrievably. She got Justice Bernard Steinmetz, a friend of Belle Moskowitz, to board the train at Harmon, where an electric engine replaced the steam engine for the final ride into Manhattan. When Smith arrived in Grand Central Terminal he had no comment for the waiting reporters.

The convention met for the last time in the afternoon to consider the Vice-Presidential nomination. Presenting Garner's name, Representative John McDuffy described his candidate as a "red-blooded he-man," and said that the ticket "brings a chill to the hearts of Republicans." "Roosevelt and Garner," he predicted, "will lead the Democratic Party to the greatest victory it has ever achieved." In a show of renewed unity, John Curry led off the seconding speeches. "This ticket cannot possibly be defeated," he said. John B. Elliott of California, in another seconding speech, drew laughter and applause when he observed that "California has had an unimportant, unassuming part in these proceedings. Californians are unassertive people."

Between the speeches, Walsh read bulletins to the delegates, telling of Roosevelt's progress. When the plane was reported sixty miles from Chicago, Walsh called a halt to the seconding speeches and announced that the time had come to vote. The balloting was monotonous and, as with most Vice-Presidential nominations, anticlimactic. Huey Long announced that Louisiana was casting its ballot for John Garner only because "it was Loosiana soldiers who freed Texas in 1836." At the end of the balloting, General Tinsley asked for a suspension of the rules and the unanimous nomination of Garner. In Washington, the Speaker listened to his nomination by acclamation in the office of Representative Lindsay Warren. It was the first time he had tuned in on the convention.

Opinion of the ticket as a whole was by no means unanimous. "It's a kangaroo ticket," said a disappointed Texan, "—stronger in the hindquarters than in the front." "Roosevelt," grumbled John McGooey, "is the luckiest man in the forty-eight states."

For two hours after the nomination the convention listened listlessly to songs and speeches, and passed resolutions of appreciation for Colonel Halsey, Mayor Cermak, Raskob, Shouse, Walsh, the ushers, and the Chicago police department. The wandering spotlights picked out Mrs. Woodrow Wilson, sharing a box with Mrs. Thomas Marshall, the widow of Wilson's Vice President, and the ladies bowed in acknowledgment of the cheers from the floor. A message was read from Senator George Norris, the liberal Republican, endorsing the ticket, and was acknowledged with thanks and some misgivings. Ex-Mayor James Curley appeared on the dais as a delegate "from the beautiful island of Porto Rico," and told the convention that there was an old Spanish custom to do something for "the forgotten man," meaning himself. As he left the rostrum, Curley grinned at the scowling delegates from Massachusetts and broke into a jig as he walked past them.

At long last the convention listened to the radio pickup of the sound of Roosevelt's plane arriving in Chicago, and the restlessness and boredom of the delegates gave way to a mood of excitement and anticipation.

As his plane left Cleveland, Roosevelt began to receive radio bulletins that the delegates were restless, and that some were going home. He began to cut his speech. On the final lap of the trip, he fell asleep. The plane touched down in Chicago just nine hours after it had taken off. Emerging with a broad smile, Roosevelt was immediately engulfed in the throng of welcomers. His hat and eyeglasses were knocked off in the crush. Spotting Farley in the crowd, he leaned over and seized his outstretched hand. "Jim, old pal," he shouted, "put it there. Great work!"

The police managed to clear a path for the beaming candidate and get him to a large white touring car which he shared with Mayor Cermak, Howe, and Farley. In the car, Howe handed Roosevelt his draft of the acceptance speech. "I sat up all night writing this speech for you, Franklin," he said. "That other one is no good. Too much Rosenman. It'll get you in wrong at the start." Roosevelt was visibly annoyed. "Damn it, Louie," he snapped, *"I'm* the nominee." But he accepted Howe's script, and when he stood before the convention, minutes later, there were two speeches in front of him.

The long route into Chicago was banked with dense crowds of cheering people. As the motorcade passed the area where the buildings of the 1933 World's Fair were under construction, Roosevelt turned to Cermak and said, "God willing, I'll be here to help you open it."*

After a short stop at the Congress Hotel, to change his clothes, the candidate pressed on to the stadium. He arrived at 6 P.M., wearing a dark suit with a red rose in the lapel, his eyes glistening with emotion. The convention gave him a roaring, standing ovation and, for once, there was not a dissenting voice in the stadium. All of the Smith diehards had left, and even the galleries were filled with admirers. That morning, Cermak had delivered thousands of tickets to Roosevelt's headquarters for distribution among the faithful.

When Walsh introduced him, Roosevelt hobbled to the lectern, aided by his son James, braced himself with his hands, and began to read, in his most beguiling voice, from Howe's draft of his speech. Raymond Moley and Sam Rosenman, standing in the back of the hall, were astounded. But after a few paragraphs, Roosevelt deftly switched speeches and read the words that he and Rosenman had fashioned:

> I have started out on the tasks that lie ahead, by breaking the absurd tradition that the candidate should remain in professed ignorance of what has happened for weeks, until he is formally notified

---

* *God was unwilling. Roosevelt was on hand for the opening of the fair, but Cermak was dead, the victim of a bullet intended for Roosevelt and fired by an Italian-born anarchist, Paul Zangara. The assassination occurred at a political rally in Miami, as Cermak stood by the side of the then President-Elect.*

of the event . . . We will break foolish traditions and leave it to the Republican leadership to break promises . . . Ours must be the party of liberal thought, of planned activities, of enlightened international outlook and of the greatest good to the greatest number.

It will not do merely to state, as do Republican leaders, that the Depression is world-wide. That was not their explanation of the apparent prosperity of 1928. If they claim paternity for one, they cannot deny paternity for the other . . . For . . . years we expanded far beyond our natural and normal growth . . . Corporate profit was enormous . . . The consumer was forgotten . . . The worker was forgotten . . . The stockholder was forgotten . . . Enormous corporate surpluses . . . went into new and unnecessary plants, which now stand stark and idle, and into the call money market of Wall Street . . .

Just a word on taxes. Government costs too much. We must abolish useless offices, merge . . . consolidate . . . give up . . . I propose that government of all kinds be made solvent and that the example be set by the President and his cabinet . . .*

This convention wants Repeal. Your candidate wants Repeal. And I am confident the United States wants Repeal . . . From this day on, the Eighteenth Amendment is doomed. . . .

I accept that admirable tariff statement in the platform. We have invited and received the retaliation of other nations. I propose an invitation to them to forget the past, to sit at the table with us as friends, and to plan with us for the restoration of the trade world. . . .

For years Washington has alternated between putting its head in the sand and saying there is no large number of destitute people who need food and clothing, and then saying the states should take care of them if there are . . .

Throughout the nation men and women, forgotten in the political philosophy of the government, look to us here for guidance and for more equitable opportunity to share in the distribution of national wealth . . . I pledge myself to a *new deal* for the American people. This is more than a political campaign. It is a call to arms.

It was a pacemaker address, rousing, crisp, full of hope and promise, and magnificently delivered. The convention punctuated its statements with roaring applause and thundered its approval at the end. The band struck

---

* *This was one campaign promise that Roosevelt never kept. In all the years of his Presidency, taxes, the cost of government, and the burgeoning of governmental offices reached unprecedented heights.*

up "Onward Christian Soldiers." John Garner sent a telegram of congratulations, saying, simply, ALL YOU HAVE TO DO IS STAY ALIVE UNTIL ELECTION DAY. Many men of conservative bent saw portents of socialism and a radical political philosophy, and were alarmed by the speech, but millions of others who heard it on radio or read it in the newspapers interpreted it as a beam of hope across a dark landscape.

Curiously, the term "New Deal" did not cause any immediate comment. It was not until Rollin Kirby, the political cartoonist, drew a picture of a farmer, resting on a plow and gazing at a lone plane in the sky, with the legend, "New Deal," that the term caught on and became the slogan of Franklin Roosevelt and his administration for all time. Actually, the expression was in fairly common usage at the time, and not merely in card games. Rosenman had plucked it out of Moley's memorandum and inserted it at the end of the speech. Roosevelt liked it immediately. He may have half remembered a letter he had received a few days before the convention began, from Thor Heydenfeldt, of Oakland, California. "Please may I suggest the following," the letter said. "Get a new pack of cards. Deal a new hand to the people. . . ."

Fifty-two minutes after Roosevelt's appearance, Madame Rose Zulialian of Massachusetts sang "The Star Spangled Banner," Chairman Walsh crashed his gavel for the last time and declared the meeting adjourned *sine die,* and the raucous, bitter, portentous Democratic Convention of 1932 passed into history.

For Franklin Roosevelt and his lieutenants, though, the struggle had just begun. Back at the Congress that evening, he had an announcement for the press: "The whole idea of flying here was to bring forward the idea of getting the campaign started. August is usually the month to get stirring, but I believe some votes can be gotten in July. The new national committee is organizing, and we start the campaign at ten o'clock tonight."

Two hours later, Roosevelt called on the national committee, meeting in the Gold Room under the leadership of its new National Chairman, James Farley. He was bubbling with plans, already busily and shamelessly trying to mend fences and bring the disaffected into his campaign:

> I had hoped to get here [he told the committee] while my old friend
> John Raskob was presiding . . . My old friend Jouett Shouse . . . Another old friend, Charlie Michelson . . . These gentlemen deserve the
> gratitude of the party. I know they would be willing to give us help
> in the campaign, and I am confident that we will have a united party
> to meet the Republican leadership.

Long after midnight, when the last well-wisher had been eased out of the Presidential Suite, Roosevelt sat up for an hour and a half, discussing campaign plans with Raymond Moley.

So Roosevelt was off and running hard, while in the White House Herbert Hoover waited to be informed that he was the Republican nominee. Happy days were still far away, but the bandwagon was rolling, the New Deal was coming, and the United States would never again be quite the same.

AFTERWORD

Chicago was as quiet as a country churchyard on the Sunday after the convention ended. On the train that took Roosevelt and his friends back to New York, there was an uproarious party, but Jim Farley did not attend. Utterly exhausted, he slept for fourteen hours. On his arrival in Manhattan, on the Fourth of July, he was refreshed and immediately went off to attend the annual meeting of the Society of Tammany, a different organization from Tammany Hall, but with the same membership. The braves were amazed to see him. "The silence that greeted my entrance into Tammany Hall was really touching," Farley recalled. But the men of Tammany shook his hand when he offered it, and through the campaign Roosevelt was given no trouble, and even got some lukewarm support, from the New York bosses.

Al Smith nursed his bitterness for weeks but kept silent. On the homecoming train, he told Baruch and Swope that he might go to Europe for the duration of the campaign. In July, though, Roosevelt and Smith met again, at New York's state convention in Buffalo, where both had gone to endorse the nomination of Herbert Lehman as governor. The meeting was cordial, and afterward Smith made a few tepid speeches on Roosevelt's behalf. Smith rode in Roosevelt's Inaugural parade, waving his brown derby and smiling broadly. But the final break between the two men came soon after Roosevelt took office, and Smith drifted to the Liberty League and the extreme right wing of politics.

Roosevelt began his campaign in August, at Sea Girt, New Jersey, at the invitation of Frank Hague—which Farley had arranged. In October,

Raskob lunched with Farley and gave him a check for $25,000—his peace offering and campaign contribution. Roosevelt made peace with Baruch, Cox, Davis, and the other men who had opposed him, but none of them ever received a favor from the White House while Roosevelt occupied it. The men who had worked to promote his candidacy, especially the early supporters and the financial backers, were all richly rewarded with ambassadorships, cabinet posts, and other high governmental positions.

In November, after a wide-ranging, coast-to-coast campaign, Roosevelt and Garner were elected in the greatest victory ever registered by a Democratic candidate—a record exceeded only by Roosevelt's reelection to a second term in 1936. Franklin Roosevelt was President for the rest of his life, through twelve hectic, historic, precedent-shattering years—longer than any other man. He was a strong president, and a controversial one. No one regarded him with neutral eyes; he was either loved or hated.

Over the years, a number of the men who had been very close to Roosevelt at the 1932 convention became disaffected and left his administration. John Garner left after two terms and went back to Texas, vowing that he would never again cross the Potomac River. He never did, outliving almost all of his 1932 contemporaries, dying in Uvalde, Texas, at the age of ninety-seven. James Farley, after serving two terms as Postmaster General, broke with Roosevelt when he sought an unprecedented third term, and went back to New York and private life. Raymond Moley quarreled with Roosevelt's economic policies and left the New Deal; the Brain Trust quickly vanished. Joe Kennedy left his post as Ambassador to the Court of St. James because he was disturbed by Roosevelt's growing involvement of the United States in World War II.

Franklin Roosevelt and the other leading figures of the convention of 1932 have all passed from the scene, except for James Farley, Sam Rosenman, and a few aging Southerners. The institution of the national political convention will probably pass into history too, before long, to be replaced by a less cumbersome, less corruptible and less colorful direct national primary election. But when the convention roll is called, 1932 will be the year and the convention to remember.

Bibliography

Allen, Frederick Lewis, *The Big Change.* New York, Harper, 1952.

Allen, George E., *Presidents Who Have Known Me.* New York, Simon and Schuster, 1960.

Burns, James MacGregor, *Roosevelt: The Lion and the Fox.* New York, Harcourt, Brace, 1956.

Byrnes, James, *Speaking Frankly.* New York, Harper, 1947.

Casey, John T. and Bowles, James, *Farley and Tomorrow.* Chicago, The Reilly & Lee Co., 1937.

Connally, Tom, *My Name Is Tom Connally.* New York, Crowell, 1954.

Farley, James A., *Behind the Ballots, the Personal History of a Politician.* New York, Harcourt, Brace, 1938.

———— *Jim Farley's Story.* New York, Whittlesey House, McGraw-Hill, 1948.

Flynn, Edward J., *You're the Boss.* New York, Viking, 1947.

Freidel, Frank, *Franklin D. Roosevelt,* Vol. 3, *The Triumph.* Boston, Little, Brown, 1956.

Gunther, John, *Roosevelt in Retrospect.* New York, Harper, 1950.

Hatch, Alden, *Franklin D. Roosevelt.* New York, Holt, 1947.

Hill, Edwin C., *The American Scene.* New York, M. Witmark & Sons, 1934.

Lawrence, David, *Beyond the New Deal.* New York & London, Whittlesey House, McGraw-Hill, 1934.

———— *Stumbling into Socialism.* New York & London, Appleton-Century, 1935.

Leuchtenburg, William E., *Franklin D. Roosevelt and the New Deal, 1932–1940.* New York, Harper, 1963.

Lippmann, Walter, *Interpretations, 1931–32,* sel. & ed. by Allan Nevins. New York, Macmillan, 1932.

————— *Interpretations, 1933–35,* sel. & ed. by Allan Nevins. New York, Macmillan, 1936.

Mencken, H. L., *Making a President—a Footnote to the Saga of Democracy.* New York, Knopf, 1932.

Mitchell, Ewing Young, *Kicked In and Kicked Out of the President's Little Cabinet.* Washington, D. C., The Andrew Jackson Press, 1936.

Moley, Raymond, *After Seven Years.* New York & London, Harper, 1939.

National Conventions of the Democratic and Republican Parties, from 1832 and 1856, respectively, comp. & ed. by Henry Harrison Smith. Chicago, The J. M. W. Jones Stationery and Printing Co., 1892.

Phillips, Cabell, *From the Crash to the Blitz. The New York Times* Chronicle of American Life, New York, Macmillan, 1969.

Rollins, Alfred B., *Roosevelt and Howe.* New York, Knopf, 1962.

Roosevelt and Frankfurter: Their Correspondence, 1928–1945. Boston, Little Brown, 1967.

Roosevelt, Eleanor, *This I Remember.* New York, Harper, 1949.

Roosevelt, Elliott, . . . *As He Saw It.* New York, Duell, Sloan & Pearce, 1946.

Roosevelt, James, and Shalett, Sidney, *Affectionately, F.D.R.* New York, Harcourt, Brace, 1959.

Roper, Daniel, *Fifty Years in Public Life.* Durham, N. C., Duke Univ. Press, 1941.

Rosenman, Samuel I., *Working With Roosevelt.* New York, Harper, 1952.

Schlesinger, Jr., Arthur, *The Age of Roosevelt,* Vol. I, *The Crisis of the Old Order, 1919–1933.* Boston, Houghton Mifflin, 1957.

Storke, Thomas M., *California Editor.* Los Angeles, Westernlore Press, 1958.

Tourtellot, Arthur, *An Anatomy of American Politics.* Indianapolis, Bobbs-Merrill, 1950.

Tugwell, Rexford Guy, *The Battle for Democracy.* New York, Columbia University Press, 1935.

————— *The Democratic Roosevelt.* Garden City, N. Y., Doubleday, 1957.

————— *How They Became President: Thirty-five Ways to the White House.* New York, Simon and Schuster, 1965.

Tully, Grace, *F. D. R., My Boss.* New York, Scribner's, 1949.

Papers and correspondence of Franklin D. Roosevelt, Louis McHenry Howe, and James A. Farley from the Roosevelt Library, Hyde Park, N. Y., and 1931–32 issues of *The New York Times, The New York Herald Tribune, The New York Daily News, Time, Liberty, The Nation, The Baltimore Sun,* and *The Chicago Tribune.*

Index

Acheson, Dean, 20
Addams, Jane, 58
Allen, Frederick Lewis, 5
Allen, George, 115
Amos and Andy, 100
Anthony, Bess Taylor, 33
Atlanta *Constitution,* 34, 41
Atlanta *Journal,* 46
Ayres, Col. Lemuel P., 77

Ballots, Democratic, first, 111; second, 111; third, 112, fourth, 123–128; Republican, 64
Baker, Newton D., 18, 19–20, 22, 34, 37, 40, 42, 47, 49, 50, 53, 77, 83, 96, 104, 105, 115, 116, 119, 120, 124, 133
Barkley, Sen. Alben B., 46, 51, 93–94, 98
Baruch, Bernard, 16, 20, 31–32, 34, 49, 77, 78–79, 93, 122 132, 139, 140
Baruch, Sailing, 77
Beauvais, Fred, 55
Beckwith, Dr. Edward W., 33
Bendix, Vincent, 78, 100
Berle, Adolph A., Jr., 40
Bilbo, Gov. Theodore, of Mississippi, 4
Bingham, Barry, 46
Bingham, Sen. Hiram, 62–63
Bingham, Robert W., 26
Boettiger, John, 69
Bonus marchers, 5–6
Booth, Evangeline, 93
Borah, Sen. William A., 72
Bowers, Claude, 55
Brain Trust, 39–41, 43, 140
Brandon, William W., 117
Brisbane, Arthur, 18, 49, 104
Broun, Heywood, 42
Brown, George Rothwell, 116–117
Browning, Edward W. ("Daddy"), 55
Browning, Frances ("Peaches"), 55
Bryan, Charles G., 11
Bryan, William Jennings, 11, 100

Bulkley, Sen. Robert J., 73
Butler, Nicholas Murray, 62
Byrd, Harry Flood, 21, 46, 53, 54, 71, 73, 95–96, 107, 109, 114–115, 129
Byrd, Adm. Richard E., 46
Byrnes, Sen. James, 46

Callahan, James M., 73
Cannon, Bishop James, Jr., 62, 97
Carter, Amon, 29, 119
Carter, Elmer A., 111
Cermak, Mayor Anton, of Chicago, 23, 47–48, 58, 68, 77, 93, 95, 124, 125, 127, 134, 135
Chicago *Daily News,* 69
Chicago *Sun,* 95
Chicago *Tribune,* 41
Clark, Champ, 20–21, 37, 75, 80, 93
Clurman, Harold, 5
Cockran, Bourke, 107
Cohalan, Daniel F., 123
Compton, Betty, 70
Connally, Sen. Tom, 29, 106, 108, 110, 116
Conventions, Democratic: Charleston, 1860, 80; San Francisco, 1920, 10; New York, 1924, 11; Houston, 1928, 12; Chicago, 1932, 92–137
Conventions, Republican: Chicago, 1920, 10; Cleveland, 1924, 11; Kansas City, 1928, 12; Chicago 1932, 57–65
Cooke, Alistair, 60
Coolidge, Calvin, 9, 10, 11–12, 23, 59, 131
Coolidge, Sen. Marcus, 47
Cotton, Hamilton, 119–120
Coughlin, Father Charles, 50, 100
Cox, James C., 10, 21–22, 23, 38, 48, 83, 89, 140
Crump, Mayor Edwin, of Memphis, 33
Cummings, Homer, 26, 54, 107
Curley, James M., 46–47, 50, 104–105, 134
Curry, John, 55, 74, 77, 105, 108, 110,

Curry, John *(Cont.)*
121, 123, 127, 134
Curtis, Vice President Charles, 12, 58—59

Dailey, Vincent, 115
Dall, Anna Roosevelt, 69
Daniell, Raymond, 57, 106
Daniels, Josephus, 81, 120
Darrow, Clarence, 32, 100
Davies, Joseph E., 26
Davies, Marjorie Merriwether Post, 26
Davis, Elmer, 42
Davis, John W., 11, 18, 22, 23, 60, 71—72, 83, 86, 89, 104, 109, 140
Dawes, Charles Gates, 11, 59
Dempsey, Jack, 27
Denegre, Walter, 101
Dewey, John, 102
Dewson, Molly, 82
Dickinson, Sen. Lester Jesse, 61
Dill, Sen. Clarence, 44, 54, 81, 90, 132
Donohue, Frank, 46—47
Douglas, Stephen, 80—81
Dowd, Tom, 55
Dowling, Eddie, 100
Doyle, Jack, 65
Durban, Col. C. W., 48
Durning, Gov. Harry M., of Kansas, 26

Earhart, Amelia; *see* Putnam, Amelia Earhart
Eisenhower, Dwight D., 131
Elliott, John, 120
Ely, Gov. Joseph B. of Massachusetts, 46—47, 55, 67, 106, 107
Evans, Silliman, 95, 115, 119, 121

Farley, James A., 17—25, 27—28, 30—31, 44, 45, 47—48, 52, 54, 55, 56, 67—69, 71—72, 80—82, 84—86, 89, 91, 95—96, 97, 98, 99, 100, 105, 108, 109—110, 111, 112, 113, 114—115, 117, 120, 121, 123, 124, 127, 129, 131, 135, 137, 139—140
Farley, Sheriff Thomas M., 69
Ferguson, Jim, 30
Fess, Sen. Simeon, 58, 61, 68
Fitzgerald, David E., 107
Flynn, Edward, 26, 54, 56, 71, 82, 108, 115
"Forgotten Man" speech, 43
Frain, Andy, 59, 64

France, Dr. Joseph Irwin, 59, 64
Fry, M. W., 30
Fuglistaler, Louis B., 28

Gann, Dolly (Mrs. Edward Everett), 12, 59
Garfield, James Rudolph, 62—63
Garner, John Nance, 18—19, 23, 34, 46, 48—49, 50, 53, 67, 71, 77, 93, 97, 101, 104—105, 106, 108, 111, 115, 116, 120, 122—123, 126, 128, 129, 131—132, 133, 137, 140; announces candidacy, 37; withdraws from race, 117—119; listens to his nomination for the Vice Presidency, 134
Garner, Mrs. John Nance, 122
Gennerich, Gus, 32
George V, King of England, 11
Gibbons, Floyd, 60
Glass, Sen. Carter, 19, 55, 82, 84, 102, 107
Glassford, Gen. Pelham, 6
Greenway, Isabella, 45, 120
Guffey, Joseph, 46, 51, 54

Hachmeister, Louise, 52
Hagerty, James, 83
Hague, Mayor Frank, of Jersey City, 49, 53, 73, 75—76, 77, 86, 99—100, 104, 106, 110, 112, 123, 132, 139
Halsey, Col. Edwin A., 101, 134
Haltigan, Patrick J., 106
Hard, William, 60
Harding, Florence (Mrs. Warren G.), 10
Harding, Warren G., 9, 10, 23, 131; death of, 11
Hargreaves, Grace Bryan, 100, 120
Harriman, Daisy Borden, 120
Harrison, Dr. J. W., 70
Harrison, Sen. Pat, 41, 46, 112, 115
Hawes, Sen. Harry B., 96, 97
Hearst, William Randolph, 18, 22—23, 37, 42, 49, 50, 55, 96, 104—105, 115, 121, 129, 130; urges Garner to withdraw as candidate, 116—117
Hertz, John D., 100
Heydenfeldt, Thor, 137
Hitler, Adolf, 1
Hogg, Ima, 30
Holloway, James C., 33
Hoover, Herbert, 3, 4, 6—7, 9, 12, 41, 42, 58, 59, 61, 62, 65; elected President,

13; renomination, 64
"Hoovervilles," 3, 4
House, Col. Edward, 47, 50—51
Houston *Chronicle,* 29
Howard, Roy, 47
Howe, Harley, 52
Howe, Louis McHenry, 16—17, 25—31, 32, 33, 39—41, 44, 46, 48, 50, 51, 52—54, 68, 82, 91, 95—96, 99, 100, 108, 114—115, 117, 118, 121, 127, 129, 132, 135
Howell, Clark, 34—36
Hughes, Charles Evans, 48
Hull, Sen. Cordell, 41, 54, 81, 98, 101, 102, 103
Hurley, Patrick J., 6
Hutchens, Robert K., 97—98

Insull, Samuel, 5

Jackson, Robert, 54
Johnson, Gerald W., 20
Johnson, Sen. Hiram, 9, 48
Jones, Jesse H., 29

Kaltenborn, H. V., 60
Kefauver, Sen. Estes, 131
Kennedy, John F., 27, 53, 131
Kennedy, Joseph P., 26, 51, 54, 74, 115—116, 130, 140
Kennedy, Robert F., 27
Kirby, Rollin, 137
Kieran, James, 40, 132—133
Kremer, Bruce, 49, 54, 81, 85—86
Kreuger, Ivar, 5
Krock, Arthur, 59, 65, 91, 102, 116, 118, 130
Ku Klux Klan, 13, 73

LaGuardia, Fiorello, 17
Landon, Alf, 16
Langer, Gov. William, of Minnesota, 3
Lawrence, David, 41, 60
Lehand, Margaret ("Missy"), 52, 91, 122
Lehman, Herbert, 51, 139
Lenahan, Mrs. W. W., 109
Leuchtenburg, William E., 2, 3
Lewis, Sen. James Hamilton, 23, 48, 71, 94—95
Lewis, Mrs. James Hamilton, 113

Lewis, John L., 19
Lewis, Sir Wilmott, 59
Liberty magazine, 42
Lincoln, Abraham, 64, 81
Lindley, Ernest K., 40
Lippmann, Walter, 19, 42, 63—64, 88
Lloyd George, David, 61
Lodge, Sen. Henry Cabot, Sr., 10, 87
London *Times,* 59
Long, Sen. Huey P., 45, 50, 74, 76, 81, 84, 86, 90, 98, 107, 134
Longworth, Alice Roosevelt (Mrs. Nicholas), 59, 93
Longworth, Nicholas, 19
Louis XV, 12
Louisville *Courier-Journal,* 26
Lucas, F. Scott, 90

MacArthur, Gen. Douglas, 6
Mack, Judge John E., 55—56, 106, 107, 108
Malone, Dudley Field, 32
Marshall, Mrs. Thomas, 134
Martin, Gen. Edward, 59
Massie murder trial, 30
Mayer, Louis B., 64
McAdoo, William Gibbs, 11, 22, 48—49, 75, 98, 103, 109, 111, 116, 117, 119—122, 127, 128, 129, 130, 132; meets with Smith and agrees to cooperate with him, 78—79; announces California's delegate-vote switch to Roosevelt, 123—126
McDuffy, Rep. John, 133
McFadden, Bernarr, 66
McGooey, John, 74, 77, 83, 123, 134
McKellar, Sen. Kenneth R., 33
McKinley, William, 8
McMasters, William, 99
McNutt, Paul V., 47, 54, 68, 114, 127
Melgard, Al, 108
Mencken, H. L., 16, 20, 42, 59, 60, 102, 113, 123, 129—130
Michelson, Charles, 88, 137
Miller, Dr. A. C., 62
Miller, Mayor Ray, of Cleveland, 19
Mills, Ogden, 62
Moley, Raymond, 40, 135, 137, 138, 140
Moody, Helen Wills, 66
Morgenthau, Henry, Jr., 26, 51
Morgenthau, Henry, Sr., 26, 31, 51

Moses, Sen. George, 73
Moskowitz, Belle, 122, 133
Mullen, Arthur, 54, 106, 112, 116, 117
Murray, William H. ("Alfalfa Bill"), 21, 53, 54, 71, 77, 83, 86, 101, 103, 111–112, 115

Nashville *Tennessean*, 95
"New Deal" origin, 136–137
New York *Graphic*, 66
New York *Herald Tribune*, 41
New York Times, 40, 57, 82, 83, 106, 123, 128, 132
New York *World*, 77
Newsweek, 40
Neylan, John, 115–116
Nixon, Richard M., 131
Norris, Sen. George, 134
Norton, Rep. Mary T., 132

O'Brien, Lawrence, 27
O'Connell, Ambrose, 123
O'Connor, Basil, 40, 117
O'Day, Caroline, 103
O'Donnell, John, 73
Olson, Gov. Floyd, of North Dakota, 3
Oulahan, Richard V., 60

Palmer, A. Mitchell, 41, 76, 98, 103
Patton, Col. George, 6
Pendergast, Thomas, 22, 45, 50, 111
Penfield, Margaret, 109
Peters, Earl, 68
Pittman, Sen. Key, 96–97
Platform, Democratic, 93
Platform, Republican, 62–64
Prajadhipok, King of Siam, 66
Prohibition, 36; Democratic action on, 101–102; Republican action on, 61–63
Putnam, Amelia Earhart, 66
Pyke, Bernice, 90

Rankin, Rep. John E., 107
Raskob, John J., 16, 21, 26, 34, 36, 37, 44, 47, 48, 49, 53, 55, 74–75, 77, 88, 90, 93, 134, 137, 140
Rayburn, Rep. Sam, 34, 54, 67, 77, 95–96, 97, 104, 105, 115, 117, 121, 123, 131–132; announces withdrawal of

Garner's candidacy, 118–119
Reed, James, 22, 31, 50, 72, 86, 100, 115, 127
Richey, Lawrence, 58
Ritchie, Albert Cabell, 20–21, 34, 37, 42, 49, 55, 71, 76, 78, 93, 95, 96, 101, 104, 107, 115, 127, 129, 132
Robinson, Sen. Joseph T., 12
Rogers, Lindsay, 40
Rogers, Will, 58, 64–65, 94, 100, 112
Rollins, Alfred B., Jr., 69
Roosevelt, Anna, *see* Dall, Anna Roosevelt
Roosevelt, Eleanor (Mrs. Franklin Delano), 15, 17, 25, 27, 30, 45, 103, 121, 127–128
Roosevelt, Elliott, 122, 127
Roosevelt, Franklin Delano, 10, 19, 20, 21, 22, 23, 25–28, 29, 30, 31, 32, 33, 34, 35, 36, 38, 39–56, 67–70, 71–77, 79, 80–86, 87–91, 95, 96, 97, 98, 99, 100, 101, 103, 104–112, 114, 115, 116, 117, 118, 119, 120, 121, 122, 123, 124, 125, 126, 128, 129, 130, 131; background and early career, 15–18; announces candidacy, 37; hears nomination on radio, 127; flight to Chicago, 132–35; acceptance address at the convention, 135–136; campaign begins, 137–38; years in the White House, 139–140
Roosevelt, Franklin D., Jr., 108, 127
Roosevelt, G. Hall, 47
Roosevelt, James (father of Franklin Roosevelt), 17
Roosevelt, James (half-brother of Franklin Roosevelt), 17
Roosevelt, James (son of Franklin Roosevelt), 46, 93, 108, 127
Roosevelt, Mrs. James, 122
Roosevelt, John, 122, 127, 132
Roosevelt, Sara, 16, 118, 122
Roosevelt, Theodore, 8, 17, 25, 56, 59, 128
Roper, Dan, 49, 54, 116, 117, 119, 120
Rosenman, Dorothy (Mrs. Samuel I.), 122, 133
Rosenman, Judge Samuel I., 39, 40, 52, 91, 122, 132, 135, 137, 140
Ross, Gov. Ben C. of Idaho, 3
Runyon, Damon, 96

Ruth, Babe, 66

Sandblast, Lawritz B., 64
Schmeling, Max, 66
Schofield, Frank, 99
Seabury, Judge Samuel, 69—70, 78, 84, 93, 105
Sharkey, Jack, 66
Sheehan, Blue-eyed Billy, 56
Shouse, Jouett, 34, 36, 49, 53, 54, 67, 73, 77, 93, 100, 110, 133, 134, 137; fight for the convention's permanent chairmanship, 88—91
Simmons, Roscoe E., 64
Smith, Alfred Emmanuel, 9, 11, 16, 17, 21, 22, 23, 31, 32, 34—38, 42, 46—47, 48, 49, 53, 54, 55, 67, 69, 71, 73—74, 75, 76—77, 83—84, 85, 88—90, 92, 93, 99, 100, 104, 105, 106, 107, 108, 109, 110, 111, 112, 114, 118, 120, 121, 124, 127, 128—130, 131, 132, 139; as the 1928 Presidential candidate, 12—13; meeting with McAdoo, 78—79; speech for Repeal, 101; learns of Garner's withdrawal, 122; bitter departure for New York, 133
Smith, Mrs. Alfred E., 74
Snell, Rep. Betrand, 61, 64
Stalin, Josef, 1
Steinhardt, Lawrence A., 26
Steinmetz, Justice Bernard, 133
Stevenson, Adlai, 131
Stiles, Lela, 52
Stillman, Anne Urquhart, 55
Stillman, James, 55
Storke, Thomas N., 119—120
Straus, Jesse, 26
Sullivan, Mark, 41, 59
Swope, Herbert Bayard, 77, 139

Taft, William Howard, 56
Talbert, Joseph ("Tieless Joe"), 61
Tammany Hall, 12, 34, 68—70, 72, 73—74, 89, 121, 123, 139
Teapot Dome, 11, 54
Thomas, Lowell, 60
Thomas, Norman, 67
Thompson, Genevieve Clark, 92

Thurmond, Sen. Strom, 131
Time, 41, 86, 106, 122—123
Tinsley, Gen. Matthew A., 132, 134
Traylor, Melvin C., 23, 33, 47, 49, 71, 95, 99—100
Tugwell, Rexford Guy, 40
Tully, Grace, 91, 122
Tunney, Gene, 100
Tydings, Sen. Millard, 20, 55

Van Buren, Martin, 80
Vanderbilt, Cornelius, Jr., 51

Wagner, Sen. Robert, 55
Walker, Mayor Frank F. of Detroit, 26, 47, 115
Walker, Mayor James of New York, 34, 47, 68—70, 78, 105, 110—111, 123
Walsh, Sen. David I., 46—47
Walsh, Sen. Thomas J., 41, 54, 87—91, 94, 100—101, 105, 107, 110, 111, 123, 124, 125, 128, 134, 135, 137
Warren, Rep. Lindsay, 134
Washington, George, 59, 93
Wheeler, Sen. Burton K., 45, 54, 75, 81, 84, 132
Whelan, Grover, 92
White, Gov. George, of Ohio, 22, 48, 71, 106
White, William Allen, 59, 129
Whitman, Charles S., 23
Wile, Frederick William, 60
Willicombe, Col. Joseph, 96, 116
Wills, Harry, 27
Wills, Helen, *see* Moody, Helen Wills
Wilson, Woodrow, 8, 9—10, 19, 41, 42, 47, 48, 50
Wilson, Mrs. Woodrow (Edith Bolling Galt), 93, 134
Winchell, Walter, 66
Woodin, William H., 26
Woodring, Gov. Harry H. of Kansas, 31

Young, Owen D., 22, 37, 49

Zulialian, Mme. Rose, 137